Finding and Keeping
Your Significant Other

Dr. Etido Oliver Akpan

A Formula for
Discovering and
Building a
Lasting Love
Relationship

Foreword by Dr. Samuel Jones
Vice President and Professor of Family Studies,
Freed-Hardeman University

ACW Press
Ozark, AL 36360

Author's note: God, Christ, Jesus, and Lord are used interchangeably in this book.

Finding and Keeping Your Significant Other
Copyright ©2005 Dr. Etido Oliver Akpan
All rights reserved

Cover Design by Alpha Advertising
Interior Design by Pine Hill Graphics

Packaged by ACW Press
1200 HWY 231 South #273
Ozark, AL 36360
www.acwpress.com
The views expressed or implied in this work do not necessarily reflect those of ACW Press. Ultimate design, content, and editorial accuracy of this work is the responsibility of the author(s).

Library of Congress Cataloging-in-Publication Data
(Provided by Cassidy Cataloguing Services, Inc.)

Akpan, Etido Oliver.

    Finding and keeping your significant other : a formula for discovering and building a lasting love relationship / Etido Oliver Akpan ; foreword by Samuel Jones. -- 1st ed. -- Ozark, AL : ACW Press, 2005.

    p. ; cm.

    Includes bibliographical references and index.
    ISBN: 1-932124-67-5
    ISBN-13: 978-1-932124-67-5

    1. Marriage. 2. Mate selection. 3. Love. 4. Soul mates. I. Title.

HQ503 .A47 2005
306.81--dc22   0509

Printed in the United States of America.

This book is dedicated to
Adrianne Akpan, the love of my life,
and to all lovers out there.

Acknowledgments

The author expresses the deepest gratitude to God for making everything possible. Several people have assisted me along the way, and many of them offered invaluable assistance without which this book would not have been possible.

My appreciations to my lovely wife (Adrianne) for her love and support. The author offers special thanks to Dr. Samuel Jones for his assistance and contribution to this book. The author is very grateful to Dr. Lela Foxx for taking the time to proofread this document and for offering useful suggestions for improving the manuscript. Dr. Akpan is extremely grateful to those who took the time to fill out his questionnaire for married couples. Many thanks to Dr. Nokomis Yeldell, Mr./Mrs. Steve and Judy Cox, Mr. James Michael Crusoe, and all others who have assisted me in one way or another during the writing of this book.

Contents

Foreword

Marriage is still very popular; nearly 90 percent of Americans expect to marry at some time in their lives. Most people enter into marriage expecting it to last a lifetime, but reality is too many marriages end by means other than the death of a spouse. Dr. Akpan, in this book, provides valuable and helpful insights for developing intimate, caring, and lifelong relationships.

Some family researchers have estimated that somewhere between one-half to two-thirds of marriages are "empty-shell" marriages. This simply means some remain in their marriage not because they are committed to it or satisfied with it, but for the sake of the children, financial stability, religious issues, etc. When the Godhead established the institution known as marriage, it was designed for couples to find joy, satisfaction, and blessings beyond comprehension. This book has been written to help couples achieve these goals.

Here is a practical resource based on experience, as well as sound educational and biblical insights. The author describes several of the most salient marital strengths and marital challenges facing couples. I am extremely pleased to recommend this book for all singles and married couples.

Samuel T. Jones, Ph.D.
Vice President for Academics and Professor of
    Family Studies, Bible, and Counseling
Freed-Hardeman University, Henderson, TN 38340

1

Introduction

"I can do all things through Christ who strengthens me."[1]

Philippians 4:13 (NKJV)

This book is based on responses from a questionnaire designed for married couples by the author. When Adrianne and I were dating and planning to get married, I was very frustrated that there was no book out there that specifically dealt with all the areas we were most interested in. As our marriage grew over the years, I pondered what could be done to assist others who might find themselves in a similar situation. That gave me the motivation to put this book together. The book provides practical steps on how to find and keep your special someone. The author highly recommends this book for all those in relationships; be it marriage, pure dating, or mere friendship with the opposite sex. The book is an immediate help for newlyweds, engaged couples, singles contemplating marriage, and struggling marriages.

The purpose of this book is two-fold: Firstly, to encourage those who have recently gotten married or have been married for some time to continue to strive to obtain the best marriage possible; and secondly, to enlighten those who are not married (singles) and those engaged to be married. The ultimate goal of the author is to help readers realize that great relationships are possible, although sometimes very difficult to build.

Relationships

How essential are relationships to us? After you ponder this question for a while, I have no doubt you will say that relationships are essential to our social and professional lives. This is especially true if you presently have or had previously experienced a very good one. Bad relationships are burdensome, but good relationships are beneficial and desirable. A relationship is unhealthy unless all the parties involved get something useful out of it.

Every relationship goes through stages. At the early stages, you are basically trying to figure out if you really like the person or not. Every romantic relationship should graduate from a liking to a loving stage. Sometimes, it takes a very long time before one can properly develop a liking or admiration for the other person in the relationship. It is possible to like someone eventually that you initially could not tolerate as you spend more time with that person. While it is necessary that you like someone to be able to get along with the person, love is what will sustain the relationship. It is often said that when you like someone, you like the person despite his or her faults; on the contrary, when you love a person, you love that individual with all of his or her faults. A lot of things will be said on love in chapter twelve of this book. The relationships we have should make our lives more meaningful, and they should challenge us to greater heights in our spiritual and physical maturity. The author aims to show the readers how to start, sustain, and maturate a relationship (particularly a romantic relationship).

Relationship and the Law of Sowing and Reaping

1. You will reap what you sow.
2. You will reap more than you sow.
3. You will reap longer than you sow.
4. Others will reap what you sow.

This law applies to all relationships, and it holds true at all times. It is the case in our relationship with God and with one another. Those in relationships should learn to sow good seeds, as these are essential to a healthy relationship. Even the smallest iota of kindness given to others, especially the significant other, will not return to you annulled. The courtesies we extend to others have a tendency to multiply when the favors are reciprocated. The things we say and do in our relationships will impact the significant other either positively or negatively.

> *The relationships we have should make our lives more meaningful, and they should challenge us to greater heights in our spiritual and physical maturity.*

When one person in the relationship gets better, the other person gets better. Anytime you take the initiative to treat your significant other better on a daily basis, he or she will respond accordingly. The positive response may not be readily evident, but you will reap the fruits of your thoughtfulness in a matter of time. If what you are reaping in your relationship is not what you want, change what you are sowing. Sow and water good seeds, and God will always give the increase. When you sow exceptional seed, you will reap exceptional return.

1. 1983. The Holy Bible, New King James Version. Nashville: Thomas Nelson Publishers

2

Communication—
the heart of a relationship

"Do not let any unwholesome talk come out of your mouths, but only what is helpful for building others up according to their needs, that it may benefit those who listen."[1]

Ephesians 4:29

Communication is one of those words that mean different things to different people, and it is sometimes misunderstood. Communication can be either positive or negative. The emphasis in this book is the cultivating of positive communications skills and the avoidance of negative communication habits. Negative communication can be just as strong as positive, but using positive language will get you better results than negative language. It is very easy to use negative language, especially when we are angry. Negative communication can create devastating problems in a relationship. In this book, positive communication is the mutual expression of one's true feeling (both pleasant and unpleasant) in a loving attitude. This can be verbal, nonverbal, or simply doing something nice for the other person. Positive nonverbal communication might include eye contact, smiling, nodding, and being at ease during the communication process. Negative nonverbal communication includes frowning, eye contact avoidance, lifeless expression, and restlessness during the communication process.[6]

There must be sending and receiving of messages, using an appropriate channel in the setting, for positive communication to be complete, and there should always be feedback from the one receiving the message. Positive communication is not nagging, getting your point across, doing all the talking, yelling or putting down the other person, giving someone a piece of your mind, or always getting the last word. Positive communication is two or more people involved in a meaningful interchange of messages back and forth; it is expressing yourself in a manner that is not hurtful to your significant other. Positive communicators tend to say the right thing the right way, and for the right reason.

Every effort should be expended to eliminate anything that might interfere with positive communication, including television, radio, interruption by a third party, and over-engagement in external affairs. While one person speaks, the other person should be busy listening and vice versa. Though most people have the ability to hear, very few possess the skill to actively listen. Unlike hearing, which most people gain from birth, listening demands hard work and a special effort to understand the other person.[5] Hearing is passive, but listening is active and involves the use of all the senses during the communication exchange.

> *Hearing is passive, but listening is active and involves the use of all the senses.*

Communication is without a doubt the very essence of relationships. A relationship depends on communication and communication depends on a relationship; this shared dependence makes it impossible to have one without the other. Communication is the very heart of all healthy relationships, and it is especially essential to romantic relationships. Romantic love demands that couples talk; when couples stop talking, they stop loving.

No one can success-fully love romantically without talking because love by its very nature communicates.

It is impossible for any relationship to start, grow, and be rightly maintained without effective communication; it will cease. No one can success-fully love romantically without talking, because love by its very nature communicates. Communication is critical, irrespective of how long you have been married or have been in a relationship. As couples become better aware of themselves, their communication ought to move from just talking about depthless things to deeper and more serious things.

Why do couples that talked nonstop while dating cease to talk to each other all of a sudden? Why do many relationships fail? Why are so many couples unhappy? Why do so many marriages end in divorce? A complete understanding of the art of communication will help one to properly answer the above questions.

Factors That Promote Good and Healthy Communication

Listening versus Hearing: The ability to really listen and not just hear the other person's voice is critical to productive communication. Being a great listener is an art and requires work. One must listen while the other person is speaking. Couples should listen without name calling and placing the blame for things that go wrong on each other. Many times, men need to be careful about offering solutions or suggestions to women aimed at "fixing things." Sometimes women want men to simply listen without telling them how to solve their problems. Superior communicators are not born; they are shaped. I am constantly working at being a better listener to Adrianne in order to improve our marital communication.

> *Superior communicators are not born; they are shaped.*

Empathy: It is essential to put oneself in the other person's situation and to treat your significant other the same way you want to be treated. Effective communication is understanding what the other person is saying the exact way it was intended, not drawing hasty conclusions, and understanding what your partner is saying before responding.

Honesty and Respect: It is important to always tell the other person how you really feel. Accurate information sharing and openness promote healthy communication. Respect for individual differences and viewpoints should constantly be maintained. Agree to disagree tactfully, and never take each other for granted.

Tone: Talking calmly and quietly facilitates good communication. Couples should express themselves carefully without using hurtful words.

Forgiveness and Forgetfulness: Be always ready to forgive and forget the wrongdoings of the other person. Do not keep a diary on how many times you have been wronged or how many times you have forgiven each other.

Time to Talk: Spouses should have a regular time, at least once a week, to talk and work out difficulties. Timing is an essential ingredient in romantic communication. You are more likely to get expected outcomes on things you want accomplished in your relationship if you pick the right time to discuss them. It, probably, will not be a good idea to bombard your significant other with series of questions and requests as soon as he or she returns from work, especially if one of you does not work outside the home. First greet your spouse, find out how his or her day went, and allow some time for rest before engaging in meaningful conversation. Couples should communicate consistently without allowing the things that bother them to build up until one or both explode in rage or become bitter or callous. When it is absolutely necessary to criticize, commence with complimentary points, and then politely bring up the one area that could improve. Be willing to admit your own faults and view constructive criticism as a positive thing. When communication problems are corrected, better relationships come as a result. Try not to retaliate with a mental list of things you also have problems with; lose the list in the first place. When one person is upset, the other should "be cool."

Promises Kept: Be a man or lady of your word. Avoid making false and empty promises. Trust, once lost in a person or relationship, is extremely difficult and sometimes impossible to regain. Never be deceptive or secretive.

Desire to Please: Work constantly at pleasing the other person before you please yourself. Selfishness is one of the greatest threats to healthy communication and successful relationship. You must learn to die to self, in a healthy way, in the interest of your relationship. The more you do for the other person, the healthier and happier the relationship. Pleasing your mate does not mean that you lose your own identity. Not only should there be a desire to please the other person, couples should always ensure that their diction or style of speech is pleasing to God.

> *Selfishness is one of the greatest threats to healthy communication and successful relationship.*

Humility: Humbleness of spirit is crucial to healthy communication. There should be humility toward God and toward each other. A concern for the spiritual health of your significant other should always be taken into consideration.

Sense of Humor: It is all right to be humorous at times, as this will contribute to an environment that is conducive to sharing of thoughts and concerns. Couples should not get so serious that they forget to laugh every now and then; laughter is nourishing to one's health and relationships. The couple must understand each other well enough for the humor to be received as intended. Having a sense of humor will dissuade couples from agonizing over minor things that do not really make sense.

Communication between Men and Women

Dr. John Gray was right when he said that men and women are so different that they seem to come from different planets.[2] Indeed, men and women communicate differently. They are different, and it would be abnormal if the differences between men and women did not manifest themselves in the ways both sexes communicate, think, perceive, and process information. The differences in communication between men and women do not only exist in social relationships, but they are also evident in professional relationships.

Because men and women possess varying mindsets, they seem to look at things from conflicting perspectives. Normally, they communicate based on their thought patterns and experiences. God must be the mediator of the communication difference between men and women. It is relevant to note that the mind controls everything else the human body does. When the mind is brought in subjection to the will of Christ, the speech will be perfectly seasoned. No one can talk and act right if he or she does not think right.

While women can easily communicate their feelings, men do not always find it easy to express their feelings. Women tend to be more emotional than men and as a result, they speak from the heart. It is common for women to initiate close ties with one another on a shorter notice than their male counterparts because they can easily share their emotions. Most men, on the other hand, speak from the head or intellect, and they appear to be emotionally sequestered.

Dr. Deborah Tannen noted that men and women communicate in different ways and for different reasons.[3] Most women prefer to talk to other women before making important decisions. Instead of talking to one another, men prefer to make decisions without consulting others because they do not want to appear weak and incompetent. Men talk more in public than women, and women talk more in private than men; this makes sense because men often communicate for status and recognition while women communicate for closeness in their relationships. A man might talk to solve a specific problem while a woman talks for understanding, support, and connection. Men and women have varying interests and as such prefer to talk about gender-specific things. Most men like to converse about sports, finances, and business-related issues; most women, on the contrary, prefer to talk about relationships, emotions, and people in general.

Most men appear to be more direct and straight to the point than most women. On the whole, women tend to be more enmeshed in details than men. Women usually stand in very close proximity when communicating with one another; they maintain eye contact, and they use more gestures. Contrary to women, men like to keep some distance when communicating with other men; they barely maintain eye contact, and they gesture less frequently.[4] It is absolutely imperative that those in cross-gender relationships, particularly husbands and wives, fully comprehend their significant other's communication style; this includes both verbal and nonverbal cues, and especially the nonverbal language. This understanding will enhance effective communication between them, and it will greatly enrich their relationship.

> *Men and women have varying interests and as such prefer to talk about gender-specific things.*

The author is not by any means saying that all men and all women communicate alike; in fact, this would conflict with the law of individuality. While all men and women do not communicate the same way, there are some general characteristics that are more prevalent and associated with one sex than the other. The recognition and complete understanding of these apparent differences are pertinent to attainment of meaningful communication between couples. Men and women in relationships should learn to appreciate each other's differences. When this is done, adaptation rather than criticism will be the ultimate focus. Although men and women communicate differently, it is fitting to stress that both styles are valid because no one way is better than the other. More will be said on men and women in chapter six.

The Tongue

Wisdom demonstrates itself in speech. The tongue can destroy a healthy relationship within seconds; it can also restore a relationship that was once broken. The tongue can do more damage to a relationship than any other organ in the body; it can create wounds that might take a lifetime to heal. The *careless tongue* will lie, curse, and utter fighting words that are harmful to the relationship. The *conniving tongue* normally gossips, slanders, and misrepresents the truth. This tongue communicates with a hidden agenda.[1]

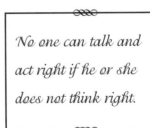

No one can talk and act right if he or she does not think right.

The two tongues described above are deadly to any relationship. The following tongues are recommended for building a lasting relationship. The *controlled tongue* knows when it is best not to say anything, thinks carefully before speaking, and normally offers wise counsel. Every relationship will be healthier if those involved know when to keep quiet. The *caring tongue* attempts to encourage; this person speaks the truth in love while building up the other person.[1] Use your tongue wisely, and you will be blessed for doing so.

Please complete the exercises at the end of the chapter.

Exercises on Communication

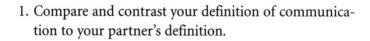

1. Compare and contrast your definition of communication to your partner's definition.

2. Do you consider yourself as a great communicator? Why or why not?

3. How often do you talk as a couple?

4. Generally speaking, what differences exist between men's and women's use of words?

5. Evaluate your communication effectiveness as a couple. What differences exist between you and your significant other?

> *A relationship ceases*
> *when communication*
> *ceases.*

6. What are the barriers to good communication?

7. Discuss the effects of the following in couple communication.

   A. Different cultural backgrounds.

   B. Different educational backgrounds.

   C. Conflicting religious backgrounds.

   D. Varied levels of maturity.

E. Outside influence.

8. Your significant other asks you: "Honey, how does this outfit look on me?" Assuming you really do not like the way the outfit fits her or him, how will you respond without concealing your true feelings?

9. Of men or women, which of the two is better at communication and why?

10. Of women or men, which one needs more communication than the other? Why do you think so?

11. List and discuss the things you and your significant other can do to improve communication with each other.

Men and women in relationships should learn to appreciate each other's differences. When this is done, adaptation rather than criticism will be the ultimate focus.

1. 1991. *Life Application Study Bible*. Wheaton, IL: Tyndale House Publishers.

2. Gray, J. (1992). *Men Are from Mars, Women Are from Venus*. New York: Harper Collins.

3. Tannen, D. (1990). *You Just Don't Understand: Women and Men in Conversation*. New York: Ballantine Books.

4. Kelley, R. H. (1996). Communication between men and women in the context of the Christian community. *Faith & Mission*.

5. Gamble, T. K., & Gamble, M. (1993). *Communication Works*. New York: McGraw-Hill.

6. www.osp.cornell.edu.

3

Is Any Relationship 50/50?

"It is more blessed to give than to receive."[1]

Acts 20:35

The conception that a relationship is and should be 50/50 is an absolute fallacy, especially to those who have at one point or another experienced the love of Christ. Life is not designed to be 50/50 and neither is a successful love relationship. In a marriage relationship, what if one becomes disabled, do you get a divorce because of that? Absolutely not. Going into a relationship with the view that responsibilities will always be evenly carried out is an illusion; it is like living in a fool's paradise because it is too far from reality. No relationship should be 50/50 if you want the best.

We live in a world that is plagued by selfishness; people in relationships are usually thinking about what they will get out of the relationships. Many go into relationships with unrealistic expectations and preconceptions. No relationship is and should be 50/50 if it is to grow to become all it can be. People in relationships change and so do the relationships. Different situations require different levels of participation, and situations fluctuate within any relationship.

There will be times you will have to give 100 percent while your spouse or significant other does not give anything at all, or vice versa. Sometimes it is 80/20, 90/10, or 50/50 on some days. Occasionally, one will give 75 percent while the other gives 25 percent. That 25 percent, as small as it is, might be just what is needed to keep the relationship complete at the time. One will always be giving or taking more than the other because one person sometimes needs more support and encouragement than the other. Every person should go into a relationship with a determination to give 100 percent at all times and receive 0 percent at times.

Everyone goes into a relationship with baggage and weaknesses. How many of us have always given 100 percent on our jobs? The appropriate response should be none because there are days we are just there and do not really feel like being there; on those days unless our coworkers step in and assist, the effectiveness of the department or organization might be in jeopardy. No one in a relationship is perfect all the time. We all mess up at one point or another. Even when we are not at our best, we still expect to be treated with love and compassion. Love should be what makes the difference at what you do. Always remember that your relationship is what you make of it. You have the power to make it the best it can possibly be.

Good relationships tend not to be too rigid; they are flexible. When there are things to be done for the betterment of the relationship, one mate steps in as needed. Couples cannot afford to only go halfway to resolve a problem or have a situation where all the work is evenly divided. Both should be willing to do whatever it takes, even 100 percent of effort or pride swallowing, to make the relationship work. Tasks to be accomplished can certainly be shared, but no logs should be kept on who is doing more or less. Selflessness and individual sacrifice are two crucial elements for a happy relationship. A marriage relationship is not intended to be 50/50 although men and women are equals. The husband is expected to bear the ultimate burden, and the wife is supposed to be a willing support system. A relationship that is 50/50 with everything will not last very long.

Just think about your relationship with God for a moment. Has it ever been 50/50? Should it be? The answers to both questions should be an emphatic no, if one is honest. We are never 100 percent effective all the time. God has always been reaching out to us, consistently making the first move, and unceasingly giving us more than we will ever be able to give Him. We will be in serious trouble if the Lord one day decides that He will no longer be nice and compassionate to us unless we give Him as much as He gives us. The Lord has perpetually treated us better than we have treated Him.

> *One must be willing to give 100 percent and receive 0 percent at times.*

What a relationship couples will have if they treat each other the same way God treats them. When couples emulate Christ instead of each other, they will often be ready to do more for the other person. In relationships, it is good to sometimes be on the receiving end. However, it is better to regularly be on the giving end because giving comes with blessings from God. Please spend some time to do the exercises.

Chapter Exercises

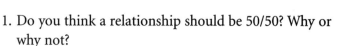

1. Do you think a relationship should be 50/50? Why or why not?

2. What do you do in a situation where one partner continually gives and is not appreciated by the other?

3. List and discuss the things you will do to improve your relationship.

4. List the things your partner can do to improve the relationship.

5. Do you withdraw more than you deposit into your relationship account? Why or why not? Examples of withdrawals are receiving more than giving and always treating yourself better than your significant other. Examples of deposits are giving more than receiving and always putting your significant other's interests ahead of yours.

6. What do you think are God's expectations for your relationship?

---

1. 1991. *Life Application Study Bible.* Wheaton, IL: Tyndale House Publishers.

4

Conflict Resolution

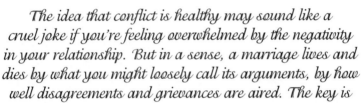

*The idea that conflict is healthy may sound like a
cruel joke if you're feeling overwhelmed by the negativity
in your relationship. But in a sense, a marriage lives and
dies by what you might loosely call its arguments, by how
well disagreements and grievances are aired. The key is
how you argue—whether your style escalates tension or
leads to a feeling of resolution.*

Dr. John Gottman, Psychologist

Conflict is a word that connotes different things to different people. Conflict denotes disharmony, disagreement, discord, contention, dispute, disunity, clash, incompatibility, dissention, faction, and strife. All relationships are susceptible to conflicts, irrespective of the strength of the union and the length of time you have been in the relationship. It is suspicious when someone says that he or she has never experienced conflicts or disagreements with the significant other. A relationship where there is no disagreement between the couple is, probably, not healthy to begin with; one person might be getting everything he or she wants while the other partner is always giving in to everything.

Frankly speaking, there is absolutely nothing wrong with conflicts or disagreements. It is what couples do with the conflicts that matters. The older your love for each other gets, the better equipped you are at dealing with conflicts. Whenever there is conflict between couples, it presents a rare avenue to demonstrate one's communication dexterity. The better a couple's communication skills, the better they are at dealing with disagreements between them. Couples should learn to talk instead of engaging in a war of words.

> *All relationships are susceptible to conflicts, irrespective of the strength of the union and the length of time you have been in the relationship.*

To some, conflicts might be seen as obstacles to the achievement of desirable goals, and to others, they might be seen as opportunities to grow and glorify God in the process of dealing with them. Conflicts enable couples to view things through the eyes of others; they compel couples to evaluate all possible alternatives and ramifications prior to making decisions affecting their relationship. There will frequently be disagreements in the family, even with couples that are very close to God. You want to resolve them using the Bible. Differences of opinion should not affect spiritual unity. If those in relationships apply the Scriptures, they will be fine at all times.

It is healthy to apply win-win strategies instead of win-lose approaches. The win-win resolution strategy continuously seeks mutual benefit of the couple involved. With this approach, the husband and wife feel good about the resolution and commitment to the action plan. This strategy

enables couples to view themselves as partners in progress
instead of competitors vying
for selfish interests. Make sure
the disharmony between you
is not due to selfishness on
someone's part. It is essential
that the two of you become
better off for going through

> *The more compromis-
> ing a couple is, the less
> conflicting the relation-
> ship will be.*

the conflicts, rather than one person being worse off than
previously. The more compromising a couple is, the less conflicting the relationship will be. Remember that God works
through conflicts.

Normally, conflicts arise when couples learn new information about their significant others, and sometimes themselves, that challenges their previously held assumptions.
Conflicts can also result when one's comfort zone is threatened, and occasionally, it can be a minor disagreement over
personal ambition, goals, or concepts. The mere fact that
men and women are vastly different creates a perfect atmos-
phere for the existence of conflicts between the two sexes. The
more a couple knows about each other, the more the possi-
bility of conflicts arises between them; and the more couples
mirror Christ, the more they will be at odds with themselves
and the better they will be resolving their conflicts. For example, if you find out new information on your partner's past that
is terribly unpleasant, it is very likely that a conflict might
ensue between you. How you deal with that new information
will hugely depend on your maturity and tolerance levels.

People in relationships should always plan for conflicts. It
is a good thing when couples take the initiative to resolve conflicts between them. Some conflicts are healthy while others are
not. Never allow conflicts to destroy your relationship. Couples

> *Sometimes, it is better to confront conflicts and other times, it is wise to avoid them.*

should embrace conflicts when they occur; this does not by any means imply that one should expend energy searching for them. Sometimes, it is better to confront conflicts and other times, it is wise to avoid them. Conflicts are not always worth the consequences. Any issue that has a significant bearing on the success of your relationship must never be avoided; it should always be sensibly discussed and resolved.

Some Things Husbands and Wives Disagree On

Money: Many couples disagree on how, when, and what to spend money on. This is particularly true during the holiday season. One might prefer to make large purchases on credit while the other likes to wait. One party may prefer to keep up entries in the checkbook while the other does not think that it is such a big deal. A couple may disagree on the use of money for clothes. Some even disagree on how much money they need to live on.

Television and Radio Programs: There are obvious differences between men's and women's program preferences. Most men like to watch sports and sometimes news while the women like to watch programs other than sports. Some enjoy talk radio while others enjoy music radio. Some do not even agree on when the TV or radio should be on.

House Temperature: Various couples, regardless of the length of time in marriage, still do not agree on the house temperature. They constantly dispute where the thermostat should be.

Exercise: A great number disagree on whether or not to give bodily exercise a great priority.

Promptness: Some do not think it is imperative to be prompt. Some believe strongly in keeping a schedule while others do not. Some like to be early for appointments while others do not.

Number, Spacing, and Discipline of Children: Many couples disagree on the number of children to have. Several couples also have difficulty agreeing on the spacing of children; one partner might want a few years between the children while the other might insist on having them back to back. Some disagree on when to talk to children about violations, and when and how to discipline. One party might prefer dealing with the violations right away while the other party might prefer to wait and think over the situation. Some simply do not agree on when children should have to take responsibility for their actions.

Vacations: Many do not agree on having a regular vacation. Even among those that agree, they still disagree on where to go on the vacation.

Where to Live: Various couples do not agree on where to live, and one person might end up giving in to the other's choice. Sometimes, a compromise that pleases both parties is achievable.

Furniture: Some couples sweat over the type of furniture to purchase and where to set it in the house.

Driving Techniques: Husbands and wives normally prefer different driving techniques. They have a tendency to criticize each other's driving.

Procrastination: Some regularly like to procrastinate while others prefer to complete tasks right away.

Movies: One might like comedy, drama, or action-packed movies while the other does not and sometimes has zero interest in any kind of movie.

Attire: Several couples still have problems with each other's style of dress or taste.

Assisting Family Members: Some do not agree on helping family members with personal issues.

Going to the Doctor: One might believe in regular health checkups while the other does not and only goes to the doctor when he or she has to do so.

Style of Relating to Others: Sometimes one is more outward with people while the other is more reserved. In my case, I have a habit of talking to strangers while Adrianne is more reserved. In private, I am more reserved than my wife.

Whispering During Worship: Many couples struggle with this because one partner might like whispering during worship service while the other cannot stand it.

Long Conversations on the Telephone: Some disagree on the length of time their spouse should stay on the telephone when talking to others. Some prefer to keep all conversations to a few minutes when on long distance call.

Cooking: Several spouses disagree on who should cook, when to cook, and what to cook.

Eating Out: Many do not see eye to eye on the number of times they should eat out in any specific period.

Bedtime: A lot of couples do not agree on the best time to go to bed.

Some Ways to Manage Conflict

Communication: This should be lengthy enough to have a complete understanding of the current problem. Every couple handles conflict poorly at first. Some pout or resort to anger at the early days of the relationship, and the anger sometimes results in a rage. Then they learn to talk things through by negotiating and compromising where no biblical principle is involved. The couple should gather the best fact and information possible, and then set up a time to talk when no one is upset. There should be open communication where both have opportunity to express themselves. There is nothing wrong with being silent momentarily if needed. Ask your partner how he or she feels and what he or she thinks. Both must really try to listen. Do not forget to make up after the discussion.

Apology: A simple apology can solve a lot of the petty things couples fret over. Some have difficulty admitting when they are wrong; no one should be too proud to admit a mistake.

Selflessness: Selfishness is the reason for many conflicts. Taking oneself out of the way and doing what is best for the relationship will bring the conflict to a speedy resolution.

Patience: Showing patience enables couples to look at the situation from both the positive and negative perspectives, thereby avoiding hasty judgment calls. Patience is a virtue that can make the conflict fade away.

Focus on the Big Picture: It is critical that couples do not lose sight of what is at stake—the relationship. Learning to ignore insignificant details will help spouses keep a good perspective on what is really important; it will also prevent couples from ruining a special moment with one another.

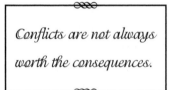

Conflicts are not always worth the consequences.

Avoid Involving Others: The fewer the number of people involved in any conflict, the quicker and easier the resolution will be. All couples should learn from the mistake of Adam and Eve in the Garden. Everything was going well between the couple and God until a third party—the serpent—was allowed into their relationship.

Prayer: Praying together can solve a lot of problems because prayer changes things. It is good for couples to stay on praying ground. Couples should always allow the word of God to be the final say; this will ensure that it is a win-win for everyone. It is relevant to be aware that emotions sometimes persist after a reasonable conclusion has been reached.

Conflict Resolution Model

The following is a conflict resolution model developed by Al Waner of California State University at San Bernadino. The model provides a step-by-step approach to conflict resolution.

Step one: Identify the conflict—what is the problem?

1. Who is involved?
2. What is the conflict?
3. When did it happen?
4. Where did it happen?
5. Resolution attempts?
6. Consequences of the conflict?[1]

Step two: Identify the solutions. What are the alternatives?

1. Develop a positive attitude.
2. Establish ground rules.
3. Identify interest of the parties.
4. Develop alternatives.
5. Identify criteria.
6. Weigh solutions against criteria.

Step three: Select an alternative—implement the action.

1. Develop a plan of action: Who is going to be involved? What is to be done? When will the parties act? Who is responsible for mediating differences (face to face)?
2. Determine how to handle the conflict in the future.

Step four: Evaluate the results of the action[2]

Step five: Move on[3]

Make a special effort to really understand where your significant other is coming from before desiring to be understood.

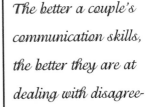

The better a couple's communication skills, the better they are at dealing with disagreements between them.

Chapter Four Exercises

1. What is your definition of conflict?

2. Can you think of a time you and your partner disagreed on the best way to complete a task? What did you do to resolve the problem?

3. How will you handle the same situation today?

4. What is your preferred style of dealing with conflict?

5. Make a list of what couples should do to resolve conflicts between them.

6. What can you learn from Christ's style of conflict resolution?

---

1. Step one: PPBS Systems. Dr. John Stallings.

2. Military model.

3. Step five: Paul, Philippians 3:13 (retrieved from http://soe.csusb.edu/awaner/conresmo.htm). Used by permission from Dr. Al Maner.

5

Dealing with Anger

Angry, cynical people are five times as likely to die before 50 as people who are calm and trusting.

Dr. Redford B. Williams

It is okay to be angry sometimes. Christ, our perfect example, demonstrated anger toward the moneychangers in the temple; God gets angry with sinful people every day. Anger is one of the basic emotions in normal people. One who says he or she is never angry is either not normal or has some other problem. The problem is not anger but its management. There is a big difference between anger and rage. Anger is synonymous with displeasure, annoyance, outrage, fury, resentment, irritation, and indignation. On the contrary, rage is anger taken to the very extreme; this is when anger becomes bad. Rage is synonymous with animosity, violence, explosion, and uproar. Expect anger to be present in a relationship. However, make sure you have a definition for it. Just like money, it is not necessarily bad, but what you do with it might be. Anger can be either productive or deadly. It can lead to hatred and murder and can also lead to an excelling relationship if it is properly channeled and effectively managed. Anger does not give one a license to be rude, slanderous, or destructive.

People get angry when things do not go their way. Anger may be caused by someone else's action or a decision you made that did not turn out the way it was expected. There is definitely nothing wrong with getting angry if that anger will cause you to do something good. Bluntly speaking, anger is justifiable in some cases. For example, one should be angry at any violation of the word of God; one should also be angry at injustice, moral degradation in society, and the dysfunction of the family. The anger must cause one to do something to improve the situation; otherwise, it will be baseless. The mission of anger is accomplished when one is moved to positively effect change. Anger, therefore, ceases to be a necessity after it causes one to do some good.

After the completion of its objective—the manifestation of good—anger becomes deadly if allowed to remain. It will cause harm because of the propensity to deplore one's life. It is impossible to live with anger and be pleasing to God. Living with anger will make you mistreat God's greatest creation—your significant other, and other loved ones. Anger will make it difficult to rejoice with those that rejoice and mourn with those that mourn. Anger can make you so dysfunctional that you become useless and burdensome to the people around you and yourself.

> *Anger can be either productive or deadly.*

Anger will cause one not to fully appreciate the goodness of God. It is impossible to live life to the fullest when someone lives with anger, as the focus changes from God to self.

Anger is not very easily controlled at times. If certain principles could be put in place and agreed on, anger can be controlled. If a couple can sense there is a great deal of anger about an issue, the couple should not try to discuss the issue at that time. Prayer and deliberation should be sought. Both should never speak at the same time. One should allow the other person to express his/her own full view of the matter, if possible, without interruption. Each person is to remember the words of Ephesians 4:26, where the Holy Spirit says, "Be angry, and do not sin; do not let the sun go down on your wrath"[1] (NKJV).

Some Ways to Deal with Anger

Time Out: Sometimes, it is necessary to call time out and back off the subject for a while, but agree to come back to talk about it after you are calm and have sorted things out in your mind. Giving yourself time to calm down will assist you in controlling your emotions. Determine if it is really worth confronting the spouse or significant other, and make sure you have factual information to share when time is right. Be certain that you communicate your thoughts politely and lovingly.

Pray About It Calmly: It is fitting to ask God for guidance and wisdom in making the right decisions. Do not forget that you are a child of God. Ask yourself this question, "What will Jesus want me to do about the situation?" Christ should always have the final say in every matter.

Confront the Problem: Do not attack the individual; attack the problem. This is not the time to discuss any other problems you may have with each other. Address only the concern at hand, and listen attentively to the response. Talk about it without the need to be right and the other person to be wrong. It may be easier to deal with the anger if you caused it than if it was caused by someone else. Even if it is not your fault, you still have obligation to God to make things right with the person. You must confront in a loving and respectful manner. Sometimes the things we think are the cause of our anger might not be accurate, so talk about the problem. The guilty party needs to genuinely ask for forgiveness and communicate clearly how he or she can prevent the situation from happening again.

Patience: Patience is needed in all conflict resolutions. It will assist one to maintain self-discipline. Patience makes it easy to think about the other person's feelings before acting. It is wise not to jump to conclusions; treat your significant other the same way you want to be treated.

Good Rules and Habits: Have some good rules and habits on how to deal with anger. For example, both of you may agree never to get angry at the same time. This rule might be unrealistic to some people, but it will work at all times if it is effectively implemented. At least one of the parties must talk and act sensibly to have a chance for any resolution. Resolve never to fall out of love with each other.

> *Living with anger will make you mistreat God's greatest creation—your significant other, and other loved ones.*

Couples should make a special effort to resolve every problem between them before going to bed. Be honest to yourself and to each other. Life is very short, and you must live each day as if it is your last day.

How to Turn Disappointments into Blessings

Recognizing the Way God Operates: It is pertinent to note that God tests our faith and sometimes uses trials to make us stronger. He will help us to understand in due time. Disappointments or problems in a relationship can build faith and character and can draw the two people closer to God and to each other. Generally speaking, Christians are tried by fire to make them pure like gold; this can also be said of a good marriage relationship. Married couples can attain via disappointments and hard times a deeper appreciation for God.

Doing for Others: Couples and Christians in general should use the experience obtained in trials and suffering to bless those who have similar problems. This will in turn bless you.

Focusing on God: God is all-seeing, all-knowing, all-powerful, and everywhere present. He understands everything that happens to His people. Put your trust and loyalty in the Lord, and keep the big picture in mind. Pray about things that disappoint you, and try to understand that there are reasons for all things. The Lord will help you make the best out of your situation. Be constantly ready to accept what God intends for you.

Looking at the Alternatives: It is good for couples to always remember that things could be worse. If it were not you, it probably would have been someone else experiencing what you are going through. Instead of saying "why me?" all the time, couples should grow enough to say "why not me?" Couples should do things together that lessen the disappointment.

Recognizing That No Problem Lasts Forever: It should be refreshing to be reminded that most conditions are not permanent. The situation you are experiencing, as complex as it may seem, will likely soon pass, and something good will come out of it. Always look on the bright side of things. See each problem as a stepping-stone to make you a better person and not a stumbling block. Realize that just because you fail here does not make you a failure. No failure is final unless you make it so.

> *"Be angry, and do not sin; do not let the sun go down on your wrath."* [1]

Identifying Causes of Disappointment: It is important to identify causes of disappointment and assess options for improving the situation. Be able to learn from mistakes, and use wisdom gained to enjoy what you have and what you can do. Be careful that you are not the reason for the disappointment.

Avoiding Unrealistic Expectation: Do not expect everything to be perfect and pleasant all the time. Life is, sometimes, not a bed of roses.

Exercises for Chapter 5

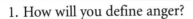

1. How will you define anger?

2. On a scale of 1 to 10, 1 being the worst and 10 being the most effective, how would you rate your effectiveness in anger management? Why do you think so?

3. What do you think are the reasons couples get angry?

4. What is wrong with anger? Explain your answer.

5. Enumerate and discuss the steps you will take to resolve anger in your relationship.

6. Are there any benefits associated with anger? Explain your answer.

7. What are the lessons from God's perspective on anger management?

---

1. 1983. *The Holy Bible, New King James Version.* Nashville: Thomas Nelson Publishers.

6

Men and Women

The differences between the sexes are the single most important fact of human society.

George Guilder

Constant kindness can accomplish much. As the sun makes ice melt, kindness causes misunderstanding, mistrust, and hostility to evaporate.

Albert Schweitzer

In chapter two of this book, communication differences between men and women were examined. Apart from communication, there are many other ways men and women differ. This chapter will explore the needs, similarities, and dissimilarities of both sexes. The chapter will also examine some of the ways those in romantic relationships can demonstrate appreciation to each other.

Men and women were created to be different. It is a great thing that both of them do not agree on every matter. Each one has what the other needs to attain the fullest potential. It will be impossible for men and women to be all that God intends for them to be unless they learn to appreciate each other's differences, are open-minded, and view the dissimilarities between them as a bonus instead of an impediment. When couples make special attempts to really understand their significant others, not only will they learn useful information, they will also realize that there is more than one way to look at the world.

Instead of wasting 90 percent of the time on the 10 percent that is wrong in your relationship, endeavor to spend the 90 percent on what you appreciate in each other. This can be very taxing if you are unhappy most of the time. However, the author strongly believes that God intended for husband and wife to be happy and satisfied in their relationship. It should be equally noted that couples have to endlessly work at making themselves happy. Not only should couples pursue happiness in their relationship, they should intensify a quest for real joy that is only found in Christ. Happiness, many times, depends on our circumstances but joy goes deeper than happiness because it fully depends on Christ. When a couple has joy, the couple will always trust in the delivering power of God regardless of the present state.

> *It will be impossible for men and women to be all that God intends for them to be unless they learn to appreciate each other's differences.*

Top Needs of a Man

His Need for God: The number one need of a man is God. This is the most essential need because everything else depends on its fulfillment. A man can live for a while without food, water, and even air, but he cannot live for a second without God. A wise man recognizes that he cannot properly function without God; he realizes that he will not even know how to lead and treat his wife and others without God. If God is not a priority, nothing else will work like it should. There will be none of the blessings (physical and spiritual) that only God can provide; no forgiveness of sin and no hope of Heaven. The need for God will always be man's most essential need, regardless of one's age or the length of time with the significant other. Many relationships and families experience trauma and breakups simply because the man has either not realized or has altogether chosen to ignore his greatest need. A wise woman will encourage her husband or potential mate to stay focused on God, realizing that the relationship cannot flourish like it should without the Lord's assistance.

His Need for Respect, Admiration, and Financial Stability: A man needs to be respected and admired by his wife or potential mate. He wants her to be proud of him, to appreciate his value and accomplishments above all others. The man wants to feel needed; he wants to feel important and not stupid. The man usually seeks respect and admiration from a relationship that has, at least, some depth. The woman knows and highly esteems her man and will do everything to protect his ego. He cherishes his woman because of her genuine respect and admiration for him. A man also has a great need to be able to provide for his family. A loss of job or other means of financial instability can seriously hamper his earnest desire to regularly provide for his family. The man's respect and admiration may be threatened when he becomes financially unstable and unable to provide for his family.

His Need for Sex: A man has a strong need for sexual fulfillment. He cannot properly operate for a long time if the need for sexual gratification is not met. God commands that this need be fulfilled in marriage. The desire for sex is so great that he must make love to his wife. The sex drive might differ between younger and older men. A good wife understands her husband's need for sex, and she continually works at being an exceptional sexual partner to him. The value of even a quick sexual session to a man should never be underestimated. The man desires his wife to be fully involved in the sexual experience. The husband and wife know what brings out the best in each other, and both of them continually strive to help each other have an experience that is thrilling, anticipated, mind-blowing, and fulfilling.

His Need for Companionship: The man needs his lady to be his best friend and lifetime partner. He wants her to enjoy or learn to enjoy recreational activities and other events with him. She endeavors to complement him by the way she dresses when they are out somewhere. The man wants them to share their experiences with each other. He desires that she keeps personal attractiveness and physique at their best. He adores her so much that her companionship means the world to him.

His Need for Family Support: A man needs his wife to support him domestically. The man realizes how extremely cumbersome it will be to attempt to achieve his goals and greatest potential without his wife's support. It is often said that behind every great man, there is a great woman. The wife helps her husband fulfill this need by providing a peaceful and quiet environment, being a good homemaker, and balancing her time between her husband and children (if any) without robbing Peter to pay Paul. She enables him to look forward to coming home after work or being away from home and understands when he is hungry or needs some space or rest. The man deeply appreciates his lady for guaranteeing him a home that encourages him to be all that he can be.

Her Top Needs

Her Need for God (Male Spiritual Leadership): Like the man, the woman's most essential need is also God. She recognizes that she cannot have a relationship that is devoid of rancor and melancholic moodiness without God Almighty. In other words, she knows that her relationship will be filled with bitterness and unhappiness without the Lord. The woman yearns for male spiritual leadership in her family to help her maintain her focalization on God; leadership driven by integrity, conviction, fortitude, devotion, and tender feeling. The wife prefers her husband to initiate things that ensure their spiritual development, and she expects him to earnestly strive to model Christ to her.

Her Need for Respect and Appreciation: The woman needs to be respected and cherished by her man. She needs personal affirmation from her husband on a regular basis without being taken for granted. The husband genuinely compliments her for her qualities as a virtuous woman. He respects and appreciates her as a wife, helpmeet, mother of his children (if any), and a great homemaker. She wants the

> *Instead of wasting 90 percent of the time on the 10 percent that is wrong in your relationship, endeavor to spend the 90 percent on what you appreciate in each other.*

husband to think the world of her. The husband appreciates and adores her so much that he is not afraid to brag on her in front of others.

Her Need for Romance and Affection: The woman wants her man to be creative and proactive in showering her with affection. She cherishes romantic surprises such as planning an unexpected meal, sending cards, flowers, and presents for no apparent reason. She appreciates a warm look and a gentle touch by her man. She likes to hear words like "Honey, I will not be as happy as I am without you" and "I love you, no matter what." The man realizes that love making for the woman starts way before getting to the bedroom, and he cannot expect his lady to turn on at night if she has been turn off all day. It is awfully difficult for the woman to be fully involved in passionate love making with her man if her needs for romance and affection are unmet. The fulfillment of these needs promotes a healthier marriage and sexual fulfillment. They are to a woman what sex is to a man.

> *It is awfully difficult for the woman to be fully involved in passionate lovemaking with her man if her needs for romance and affection are unmet.*

Her Need for Intimate Communication: A woman has strong need for intimate communication with her man. She expects her husband to communicate to her at the emotional level, by actively listening and not just hearing. Intimate communication is believed to be the way to a woman's heart. The woman wants him to spend enough time to really know her

heart without attempting to
change who she is. He makes a
special effort to really understand where she is coming
from by paying attention to
both verbal and nonverbal
languages in order to increase
sensitivity to her desires. The
woman's need for intimate
conversation is so great that
she cannot go very long without talking to someone. When

> *The woman wants him
> to spend enough time
> to really know her
> heart without attempt-
> ing to change who she
> is.*

this need is not met, she might have a tendency to seek out
others who are willing to listen to her need. The husband
knows his wife well enough to understand that her need for
communication is greater than his, and he will do everything
within his power to help her fulfill this great need.

Her Need for Security, Fertility, and Companionship: A
woman needs protection, a sense of safety, financial and
emotional security, and companionship. She needs to feel
safe with her man. The loving husband will consistently make
sure that his wife feels protected and is provided with all of
life's basic necessities throughout her life. He does not see
doing for her as a burden but as a chance to thank God for
her. The man takes his responsibility as the security hub of
the family with all seriousness; by doing this, he vividly
demonstrates an undaunted commitment to his family.

Most women feel it is natural to be able to bear children.
So many women are unhappy when this need is not fulfilled.
If the woman cannot bear children, she might feel that she
has let her man down. Only a close and daily walk with God
and her husband can relieve this pain of inability to conceive

and bear children. In a time like this, her man's companionship means everything to her. A couple may consider alternate forms of parenting like adoption. The woman is naturally the weaker vessel (physically speaking) and as such has a great need for her man to continually be by her side to encourage and reassure her and to give her a sense of belonging.

Some Ways Men and Women are Similar

1. Both men and women need God, to be loved, and to be understood.
2. Christian men and women have the same spiritual goal of making Heaven a home.
3. They both like respect, attention, and thoughtful gifts.
4. Both are hurt by harsh words and want to be happy.
5. Both need food, rest, and to live in reasonable comfort.
6. Both have physical, emotional, and spiritual needs and wants.
7. Both need praise, recognition, and encouragement.
8. Both need space.
9. Both want to feel appreciated, wanted, and valued.
10. Both normally want children and are nurturing and protective of their offspring (if any).
11. Both seek to leave a legacy for their children (if any) and others.
12. Both honestly desire to please their mates.
13. Both enjoy lifelong companionship of the opposite sex.

Some Differences between Men and Women

1. Most men speak from the head (facts) and most women speak from the heart (feelings). Men want to deal with facts, and women want to deal with feelings.

2. Women tend to be more emotional and more sensitive than men. While women express their emotions more often, men tend to internalize their feelings and are less perceptive of others' feelings.
3. Men normally have a higher sex drive than women.
4. Men and women normally like different television programs.
5. Men typically do not like to be told what to do, and women do not like to be put down.
6. Most women enjoy shopping more than men.
7. Women are more talkative and more easily offended than men.
8. Men will often times worry less than women.
9. Women generally like to share their problems with others, and men normally prefer to deal with their problems alone.
10. Men, on the whole, are more aggressive than women.
11. Women, many times, are more spiritual than men.
12. Women frequently are more able to sustain and value relationships; they seem to be more nurturing than men.
13. Women, for the most part, hold grudges longer than men.

How He Can Show that He Loves Her

1. Support her endeavors.
2. Compliment her regularly; tell her what she does well.
3. Do things that make life better for her.
4. Seek to do things that please her.
5. Serve and minister to her needs.
6. Show honor and respect: never criticize her publicly; lift her up.

7. Talk to her about how much she means to him.
8. Spend time with her without the interference of others.
9. Support her emotionally, financially, and spiritually.
10. Protect and be faithful to her.
11. Tell her he loves her on a regular basis.
12. Speak her love language.
13. Pamper her with affection. Never forget to do the little things for her like opening the car door and roses for no reason.
14. Be understanding and patient with her, recognizing her emotional and sometimes complicated nature.
15. Ensure the family stays faithful to Christ in every way.
16. Encourage her to be the best she can be.
17. Ask her what he can do to fulfill her needs.

How She Can Show that She Loves Him

1. Be faithful to him.
2. Greet him lovingly when he comes home.
3. Prepare his favorite meals. There is a saying that "the way to a man's heart is his stomach."
4. Praise him regularly; accentuate the positives.
5. Encourage and support him in his work. Live within his means.
6. Do things that make him happy.
7. Clean the house and be a good homemaker. Take care of the things he provides.
8. Always look good for him; dress to complement him.
9. Respect and honor him by obeying him in the Lord and expressing confidence in his leadership. Do not compare him to other men.
10. Make a special attempt to truly understand him.
11. Care for his offspring (if any).

12. Be his biggest cheerleader.
13. Ask him what she can do to help him be all that he can be.

Exercises for chapter six

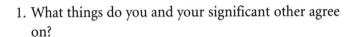

1. What things do you and your significant other agree on?

2. What things do you and your significant other not agree on?

3. How do you deal with your differences?

4. How can you bring out the best in each other?

5. What attracted you to each other?

6. Are you still attracted to each other the same way and for the same reasons you were when you first met? Why or why not?

7

Before Saying "I Do"

Love is the only spiritual power that can overcome the self-centeredness inherent in being alive. Love is the thing that makes life possible, or, indeed, tolerable.

Arnold Toynbee

Marriage is one of the serious reasons for courtship. It should not be based on lustful thoughts alone without commitment to God and to each other. Love should be the overriding reason for wanting to get married. There should be first of all a love for God and then a love for each other. You are not ready for marriage if you do not know God's will on marriage.

Although there is no real time limit on how long one should date before marriage, the author recommends that the dating period should last at least one year. Singles contemplating marriage should date long enough to really know where the potential mate's mind is; most successful married couples I spoke to said that they dated for at least one year, which is the time period Adrianne and I dated before getting married.

After one year, you should have had ample opportunities to know enough to more accurately tell where his or her mind is. The true person is normally revealed by constantly asking relevant questions and by talking about essential matters; the mouth usually speaks the overflows of the heart.

Divorce is only good before marriage. Given the seriousness of marriage, it is imperative that you do your homework before saying "I do." Prepare yourself to be an exceptional marriage partner before you choose. Marriage is not only about marrying the right person; it is being the right person. You have to be right kind to attract the right kind. Be absolutely certain that you are what you are looking for; in other words, evaluate yourself using the same criteria and standard you use to evaluate your potential mate. Use the word of God as the ultimate standard.

> *Divorce is only good before marriage.*

Some Issues You Should Address

God and Religion: It is absolutely necessary that you discuss God and religion prior to marriage. How important is God and using the Bible as the ultimate standard in your life? Are you of the same faith? What belief systems do you have? Do you have spiritual goals for yourselves and the marriage? How much time will you spend each day with God? Have you decided where you are going to be worshipping? How do you feel about regular church attendance? Are you sure you are spiritually fit for each other? What is your concept of Heaven and Hell?

Marriage: What is your understanding of marriage? Have you been married before? If so, were you scripturally divorced? Is there anything in your past that might be a hindrance to this relationship? Why do you want to be married? Why do you choose this person to be your mate? Do you believe in the permanence of marriage? How do you feel about faithfulness to the spouse and marriage vows at all times? Are you committed to this person for life, no matter who comes along or what happens? What will you do to make your marriage work?

Money: Who will be financially responsible for the general household? Are you financially ready for marriage? Do you have any unpaid debt? If so, how are you planning to pay it off? Will you have joint or separate accounts? Who will be making sure every bill is paid on time? How much money do you intend to make? Do you have a budget? What agreements have you reached to help you stay within the budget? Is it necessary to always consult your mate-to-be before making any purchases, especially expensive items? How much money is acceptable to spend without consulting your mate? Will the wife work outside the home? How often will you eat out? Many marriages end in divorce because of money problems.

Sex: How do you feel about sex? How often are you planning to have sex with your partner? Do you prefer setting up specific times for sex or engaging in it at the spur of the moment? Are you willing to make any necessary adjustments to improve your sex life? Have you ever been tested for sexually transmitted diseases and other things that may have a bearing on your sex life?

Leisure Time Activities: What do you like to do in your leisure time? Do you know where holidays and vacations will be spent? Are you willing to try new things with your mate to be?

Children: How do you feel about children? Are you planning to have any children? If so, what is the spacing between them (if you have more than one child)? Are any outside children involved? What goals do you have for the children? Will you send them to private or public schools? What will you do if you cannot have biological children? Will you be willing to adopt? If so, what criteria will have to be met prior to any adoption? What will you do if your children want to date or marry someone from another race or culture? Do you have hereditary problem that may affect your children?

Parenting: How do you feel about disciplining your children? Have you agreed on the method of discipline? Who will do the disciplining of children? Were you spanked as a child? Is spanking acceptable to both? Couples can experience all kinds of problems if one believes in discipline and the other does not.

In-laws: How do you feel about your potential in-laws? Do both of your parents agree to your marriage? If not, what reasons do they give to discourage your marriage to each other? Are they legitimate reasons? If so, have you addressed them? Do you have serious problems getting along with them? How are you planning to deal with them after the wedding? Do you have any family background issues? Are you planning to involve in-laws in resolving any marital problems? How will you resolve problems with in-laws? What are some of your family traditions? Will you continue these traditions in your new relationship? How does your significant other feel about the traditions? A lot will be said about in-laws in chapter eleven of this book.

The Design of the Family: What does it mean to be the head? Does one have any problem being submissive? Do you agree on God's design for the family? What are the roles of husband and wife? What do you expect your roles to be in the marriage? How do you view role sharing between husband and wife? If you agree on sharing roles with your spouse, which ones would be shared? What is your concept of an ideal family? How do you feel about extended family? Christ cannot be the head of the family unless the family completely submits to His lordship. More will be said on God's design for the home in chapter thirteen.

Family Devotions: How do you feel about daily family devotions? Do you see family devotions as a necessity? Have you agreed on the time for your daily family devotions? What will you do if the telephone rings or someone is at the door during the devotion? Family devotions provide unique opportunities to spend time with God and to fellowship with your family.

Place to Live: Do you know where you will live after the wedding? Are there things about the place to live that one of you has issues with? If so, have you thoroughly addressed those issues? What is your idea of a dream house?

Relocation: Have you talked about relocation should that be warranted? Under what circumstances will you agree to relocate? Are there places you would not like to live? If so, which places? Have the two of you agreed on this?

Previous Relationships: Have you talked about old friends (ex-girlfriend or boyfriend), current, and future friends? What will be their place in your new relationship? How have you demonstrated commitment and loyalty in past relationships? How do you feel about a married person having a friendship with the opposite sex?

Habits: Do you have any personal habits that might cause some problems in the marriage later on? Does your potential mate have habits you cannot stand? Is either of you quick-tempered? If so, have you fully reached a resolution on these matters? It is fair to stress that little and often ignored problems during dating periods can become serious problems after the wedding.

Goals and Interest: Have you shared your personal and professional goals with each other? What are your goals and dreams? What does your potential mate think about your goals and interests? What will you do to actualize your goals and interests? Will the goals and interests help or hamper your relationship?

Likes and Dislikes: What are your likes and dislikes? What do you have in common? What attracted you to each other? Do you or your potential mate have any pet peeves that might create some problems in the relationship? If so, how do you plan to deal with them? Do you think you will change your would-be spouse for the better after the wedding?

Lifestyle: Have you discussed your preferences when it comes to lifestyle? Do you think you can afford the lifestyle that you choose to embrace? What does God say about your preferred lifestyle?

Advice for the Engaged Couple

1. *Make sure you have premarital counseling.* Do not settle for any counselor; pick a Christian counselor that is highly skilled in premarital and marital counseling, and one that is successfully married as well. The counselor

must be able to help you understand the seriousness of the decision you are about to make. The most crucial decision anyone will make, apart from the decision to obey the gospel, is one of choosing the person to spend one's life with. This decision may determine where you spend eternity. Do not ever feel that you have discussed or talked about everything. People should want serious questions raised by the counselor to really cause them to think. God should always be at the center of a hope for a viable marriage. Premarital counseling is essential and helpful in assessing your readiness for marriage.

2. **Take all the time you need.** It is wise for couples to date for a long time before marriage. Get to know all you can about the one you are going to marry – his or her family background, work ethics, health, credit history, sexual history, criminal record, and faithfulness to Christ. Observe your potential mate in all situations requiring various aspects of his or her character.

3. **Be absolutely sure this is the person you want to spend your life with.** Do you love this person enough to stand by him or her, no matter what occurs? Do not marry someone you do not like. Do not get something started with someone that is not right for you. It is always easier to get a relationship started with someone than to get out of one because of emotional attachment and some people's unwillingness to let go.

> *Marriage is not only about marrying the right person; it is being the right person.*

4. Marriage is a full-time work, and it is not for those who are seeking part-time employment. You have to daily work at having the best marriage. Anything as great as marriage is worth working on. The best things in life are not free; you have to work to obtain them. Nothing is free, even in Freetown.

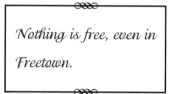

Nothing is free, even in Freetown.

5. Avoid the temptation to move in with someone prior to marriage; this is morally wrong. Such a practice will not speak well of you.

6. Make sure you have your own place to live after the wedding. Remember, you must leave before you cleave.

7. Plan for a honeymoon you can afford. Do not try to keep up with the Browns.

8. Avoid unrealistic expectations. Examples are: thinking that your would-be mate is perfect and can do no wrong, and thinking that you will always be happy. Expect ups and downs, but anticipate the downs to evaporate with a little effort and attention.

9. Do not please others at the expense of each other. Your significant other should be second only to God on your priority list.

10. Keep no secrets from each other. Be willing to discuss all the secret things that might affect your marriage to each other.

11. Be extremely prayerful.

12. It is not necessary to like all of the same things. Be open to support the other's activities.

13. Always treat your mate the same way you want to be treated.

14. Do not judge harshly. Be understanding, patient, loving, encouraging, and courteous.

15. Cultivate a strong and healthy sense of humor. Do not spend all your energy on things that threaten to keep you apart.

16. Be best friends. Best friends will not mind going the extra mile to protect each other's interest.

17. Always be willing to talk about the things that bother you. Communication is the gateway to intimacy. Note that marriage alone will not eliminate loneliness.

18. You must have God as the foundation. This is crucial because it is impossible to know everything about your potential mate prior to marriage. Go into the marriage believing that God will help you work out any difficulty. Resolve to work through whatever you are faced with. With each successful resolution comes a richer, deeper love, and appreciation for each other.

19. Be slow to anger and be quick to forgive.

20. Pick someone who is complementary to you; someone who will encourage you to attain your greatest potential.

21. *Marry someone who will help you get to Heaven.* This means the person must be a faithful Christian. Do not sell your soul for a husband or wife; protect your soul because it is the most valuable possession you have.

Chapter Exercises

1. What is marriage to you?

2. Why do you think you are ready for marriage?

3. Why do you think this person is right for you?

4. Why do you think you are suitable for this person?

5. How much do you
know about his or her
family background?

> Marriage is a very
> serious business, and it
> is only for those who
> are prepared for the
> responsibilities that
> come with it. Prepare
> yourself to be an
> exceptional marriage
> partner before you
> choose.

6. Do you have a financial plan? If so, describe it.

7. What will you do to stay within budget?

8. What are you doing for your honeymoon?

9. Where will you live after the honeymoon?

10. List all the things you honestly appreciate in this person.

11. List all the things you dislike in this individual.

12. How will you deal with conflict in your relationship?

13. Will you be a committed caregiver by patiently assisting and cleaning up after this person if he or she is seriously sick?

14. Where do you plan to be in your relationship five years from now?

15. Evaluate your relationship with God.

16. How committed to God is your would-be spouse?

17. Will this person help you get to Heaven? Why or why not?

> *Marriage is a fulltime work, and it is not for those who are seeking part-time employment.*

8

Marriage, Divorce, and Remarriage

"Marriage is honorable among all, and the bed undefiled; but fornicators and adulterers God will judge."[1]

Hebrews 13:4 (NKJV)

"Have you not read that He who made them at the beginning made them male and female; and said, For this reason a man shall leave his father and mother and be joined to his wife, and the two shall become one flesh. So then, they are no longer two but one flesh. Therefore what God has joined together, let not man separate."[1]

Matthew 19:4-6 (NKJV)

Marriage

The goal in this chapter is not to offend anybody but to encourage us to go back to God's original intention for marriage. Marriage is a God-ordained union between one man and one woman for life. As God's institution, it should be entered with the highest degree of seriousness. It is sacred and binding. Marriage is something you do for yourself. You do not marry for Mom and Dad or any other person. You marry for yourself; you marry this person because the individual is good for you; you marry this person because he or she will assist you get to Heaven.

Marriage involves first of all leaving parents before cleaving to the spouse. Sometimes, one has to leave the physical to cleave to the spiritual. When a man and a woman get married, a covenant is immediately established before God and between them. Marriage pictures Christ's relationship to the Church, and it provides the best condition for raising children. Your spouse should always be your best friend because a friend loves at all times. However, the goal of marriage should surpass that of friendship; it should be oneness (one flesh) as was intended by God. The ultimate goal of marriage should be to honor and glorify the Lord in that union. Oneness in marriage is not limited to sexual union, and it does not mean that husband and wife will always think alike or agree on every thing; it implies that they should be unified in recognizing the word of Christ as the absolute, authoritative, and objective standard in marriage.

Engaging in a wrong marital relationship is spiritually detrimental, irrespective of all the pleasures of the world that may bring. A wrong relationship is one that Christ does not authorize in His word. Be extremely careful about being caught up in mixed marriage or an adulterous relationship; God has repeatedly warned against Christians marrying non-Christians and against marrying someone who is not scripturally divorced. It is very easy to trivialize religious differences when engaging in a relationship. Apparently insignificant differences can have a devastating effect on a marriage. It is suitable to say that those couples who have successfully converted their significant others are an exception to the rule rather than the norm.

Even when you choose someone of similar faith, do so very cautiously. Be sure to do your assignment, and remember that simply being of the same faith does not make you right for each other. Do not be made to believe that everyone in the Church is spiritual. Everyone in the Church is not spiritual because people are always at different levels of spiritual maturity. It is, therefore, imperative and beneficial for one to always follow God's standards in all relationships, and especially in a marriage relationship.

Marrying someone from the same faith will save you a lot of headaches. Marriage in itself is not easy to build. It is more difficult to deal with problems when a Christian marries a non-Christian. The unbeliever can easily lead the believer's mind away from serving God. One might be trying to do right while the other is unconcerned. You have two different minds with conflicting focus, priorities, and standards of right and wrong. Two God-fearing people should frequently be willing to work out any problem with each other. Married couples have a responsibility to bless one another's life with their love. Love is an active word that demonstrates itself in action, and it seeks to do for others what it wants for itself. A lot more will be said about love in chapter twelve of this book.

Do not ever underestimate the influential power of the person you are in love with. He or she can influence you to do things you would not otherwise do. Because you want the relationship to work, you are

> *It is very easy to trivialize religious differences when engaging in a relationship. Apparently insignificant differences can have a devastating effect on a marriage.*

willing to give all you have, sometimes even compromising your principles. Marrying someone from a different faith will not only create huge problems for you, but it will create more problems when children are involved. There will be split loyalty, as both parents will be fighting to secure the children's loyalty. When we do things God's way, they will always turn out right.

Divorce

It was noted in the previous chapter that divorce is only a good option prior to marriage. After the wedding, divorce quits being a desired alternative. In preparing for the marriage, the two people must be sure that their love for each other is genuine and that their love is sufficient to stand the stress of strong disagreements that might occur.

If any couple reaches the regrettable conclusion that divorce is a necessity, three questions should be raised:

1. Have we sought every avenue to solve our differences without going to the divorce court?
2. Are we divorcing for a scriptural reason?
3. After divorce, then what?

There can be many problems after divorce depending on whether or not children are involved. If so, how do they handle the matter of the former spouse being involved in case they enter into a second marriage?

There is the problem of child support that could raise serious issues and have unsolved problems in the second marriage, knowing that funds have to be taken from the second marriage to support children from first marriage when the husband is the basic breadwinner. In some cultures, it might be that ex-wife might need to give child support. It is known that the ex-mate being in contact with a former partner can create problems with the present husband or wife.

When we look at God's view of divorce, it is evident that the Lord hates divorce—Malachi 2:14. Christ declares in Matthew 19 that He does not endorse divorce unless there is biblical ground for it. Even then, it is believed to be God's will that forgiveness and continuation of the marriage will be the best solution, if the innocent party can deal with the extreme matter of infidelity. There has been a report of several polling of all the people who were asked about divorce and remarriage; at least 70 to 75 percent of them said they would not divorce again if they had to do it over. Divorce leaves a lasting mark on not just the two parties, but it can also be a catastrophic blow to the children, if the couple has any children. Every child has a right to be brought up by two loving parents.

The author believes that if two Christians in a marriage follow God's rule, there will be fewer divorces. If Paul's admonitions to the Corinthians in 1 Corinthians 7 were adhered to, that every man has his own wife and every woman has her own husband, divorce would be extremely unlikely. It is believed by many that financial difficulty is one of the paramount reasons for divorce. More will be said on how to stay out of money trouble in chapter ten of this book.

> *When we do things God's way, they will always turn out right.*

Remarriage

In America today, more than two million couples get married every year. However, studies reveal that close to half of these marriages are people getting married for second, third, or even fourth time. This demonstrates that in too many marriages, the love and thrill that once existed do not last.

In God's order of things, marriage is for life. There are only two allowances for remarriage—if the previous marriage ended because of adultery or infidelity, and then only the innocent party is permitted to remarry; the other allowance is the death of the previous spouse, which automatically frees one to remarry. The Apostle Paul did not contradict or add any other reason in 1 Corinthians 7:15. Some divorce and remarry using irreconcilable differences as an excuse. This is a false assertion because every difference is reconcilable if the two people in a relationship are willing to make some changes.

> ∞
>
> *Engaging in a wrong marital relationship is spiritually detrimental, irrespective of all the pleasures of the world that may bring.*
>
> ∞

Death and adultery are the only scriptural reasons for remarriage. No amount of battling with the Bible will ever change what Christ had said on remarriage; it does not matter how sad or unfair one's situation may be. Therefore, think and rethink; then choose carefully who you want to marry. Never look for excuses to leave your spouse; prepare to live with your choice for life.

Four Essentials to a Lasting Marriage

1. *Trust:* Normally when people have any problems in life, they usually go to the ones they trust. Trust is in fact the basis of any relationship, and particularly a marriage relationship. The most essential ingredient in the family is forgiveness, and the next is trust.

2. Faithfulness: It is critical that couples stay faithful to each other and to God. This is solely for the husband and wife, and no one intrudes on it. It is so hard to forgive this because the damage has been done. You can easily forgive other sins but not the sin of unfaithfulness.

3. Commitment: Couples must be willing to show a commitment to God and to each other. If there is no commitment, the marriage is bound to fail. There must be a lifelong commitment for the marriage to last. A successful marriage does not just happen, but it is built on a solid foundation. Simply because a couple has been married for years does not guarantee that the couple will continue to stay married, and merely because a couple just got married does not mean that the marriage is bound to fail. The only thing that guarantees that your marriage will last is having a daily personal relationship with God and always allowing Him to have His way in your relationship. You commit first to God, then to each other.

4. Forgiveness: Forgiveness is one of the keys to a healthy and lasting relationship. One of the pointless destroyers of relationships is lack of forgiveness. Asking for and giving forgiveness are crucial in any relationship, and especially in a marriage relationship. Frankly speaking, forgiveness is really something you do for yourself; it is a present you give to yourself. Forgiveness is not a feeling; it is a decision, though very difficult at times. You forgive because you realize what is at stake. A forgiving spirit depicts spiritual and emotional maturity. Forgiveness keeps the door to intimacy and connection open. Unforgiveness can cause one to be very bitter and unable to give or receive love. Forgiveness is the most essential ingredient in the home; without forgiveness, it will be impossible to have a successful relationship. This is so because no one has ever been perfect at all times; couples wrong one another on many occasions, and forgiveness remains the only hope for sustaining a marriage and mending broken relationships.

Some Things You Can Do to Keep Happiness in Your Marriage

1. *Work at making each other happy.* Consider what puts your spouse on cloud nine and make that a priority in your life, even if you do not care very much about these things.

2. *Recognize that you are two different people, although you are one flesh.* Instead of spending all your energy trying to change your mate, spend the same amount of effort on changing you, and you will be happier as a result. It is often said that opposites attract. Why should this change after you get married? Love can agree to disagree. Irrespective of what your differences are, you should always be willing to yield to God's standard of right and wrong.

3. *Keep communication lines open at all times.* If the communication line is closed, the relationship will instantaneously be placed on life support. Unless communication returns immediately, the relationship is bound to die. Just like the body needs food and water, relationship needs communication to live.

4. *Do not sweat the small things.* Overlook the little things that might bother you, realizing that your spouse does

not intend to hurt or offend you. Handle the small things properly and the big things will be easy.

5. *Avoid unhealthy habits like telling jokes your spouse does not think are funny or always being overcritical.* Build each other up at home and away from home; do this in the presence of your family members (in-laws) too.

6. *Love each other passionately.* Be always willing to give and receive love. Remember, "...love will cover a multitude of sins" (1 Peter 4:8 NKJV).[1] Do not forget to kiss each other.

7. *Do a lot of things together.* This will keep courtship alive. Be eager to spend some time together in praying, singing, studying, and playing.

8. *Focus on the good things about each other.* Compliment each other both privately and publicly.

9. *Have a healthy sex life.*

10. *Give presents to each other.*

11. *Always remember that you are the key to your happiness.* Do not allow anyone to snatch your joy from you. True happiness comes from learning to give more than you want to receive.

12. *Always serve God and each other.* Be always ready to serve your spouse before you serve yourself.

13. *Do more than expected.* It is all right to go the extra mile for each other.

14. Be considerate of each other. Being extraordinarily kind to your mate can cause a positive and drastic change reaction for the betterment of your relationship.

15. Do not harbor grudges or unhappy feelings. Deal with them if they are legitimate concerns or better yet, trash them on a daily basis if they are not significant.

16. Keep your honeymoon breathing. There is nothing wrong with going on a second, third, and even a fourth honeymoon if you are financially able. It is also perfectly normal to renew your vows to each other regularly.

17. Be content with God and each other.

18. Be intentional in creating happy memories. Remember that the things you do today will be all you have to look on tomorrow.

19. Resolve not to allow anything to separate you. Husband and wife ought to be so close that they are virtually inhaling the air that each exhales.

Some of the Most Joyful Moments in a Marriage

1. The security of knowing that someone loves, cares, and is there for you no matter what happens.
2. Resolution of conflict and making up after an argument.
3. Spending quality time meditating on God's blessings, and sharing the day's activities together. This offers opportunity to share the love and affection you have for each other.
4. Serving God together; worshipping and visiting the sick.

5. Lovemaking. This is an experience God puts in marriage for couples to enjoy.
6. Sharing your accomplishments with each other.
7. Birth of children and grandchildren.
8. Watching a child mature.
9. Special dates together.
10. Giving gifts for no reason.
11. Celebrating the achievements of children and grandchildren.
12. Witnessing children and grandchildren give lives to Christ.
13. Marriage of a child or grandchild to a Christian mate.
14. Settling into a new home.
15. Sharing responsibilities together.
16. Vacationing together.
17. Renewing of marriage vows after several years with each other.
18. Observing spiritual development in spouse and children.
19. Supporting each other in personal and professional interests.

Some of the Saddest Moments in Marriage

1. *When communication and understanding break down.* You cannot have a happy marriage without talking to each other. When communication stops, it is normally a result of unresolved conflict or anger. Resolve every issue you have before going to bed.

2. *When you are away from each other.* This will depend on the kind of relationship you have with each other. If you are generally unhappy in your marriage or your spouse does not treat you right, you may be glad to be away for some time.

3. Marital unfaithfulness; this leads to a loss of trust.

4. Hurtful words uttered during an argument. Be careful about the things you say to each other when you are angry. The effect of verbal abuse on a man is as damaging as the effect of physical abuse on a woman. Avoid verbal, physical, and emotional abuse of each other. Do not use intimate knowledge you have of each other against each other during an argument.

5. Forgetting a birthday or anniversary. Women tend to be sadder than men when it comes to this.

6. Disrespecting and ignoring the spouse.

7. Allowing the thrill that once existed to die. You cannot afford to let your first love die. If you do, you will be a very sad couple.

8. Protracted illness: This can be terribly hard on a family. It is awfully difficult to watch your loved one(s) suffer.

9. Death of a spouse, child, grandchild, or any close family member. The death of a mate is the greatest and most painful loss any spouse will ever experience. In a time like this, only God can comfort the one who is left behind. You will never know what it feels like until you actually experience it. The death of other family members can also destabilize a family. Death is a loss that is both irreparable and tragic. It is good for a couple to recognize the brevity of life and to make the best of their time with each other.

10. Loss of a job. This can be very difficult to deal with, especially when you are the primary bread winner and bills are coming in at the same time. The only thing that makes the difference is a total dependence on God Almighty. In my case, I lost my job two weeks after closing on our first home we are still living in at the moment. I had to learn that worrying will give one something to do, but it will not take one

> *Failure and disappointment come our way to help us realize our limitations and frailties, and the need to always rely on Christ.*

anywhere desirable. Do not be the reason you are losing the job; never quit what you are doing till you find a better job. If you lose a job for reasons beyond your control, do not live like one without hope. Put all your hope and trust in Christ, and He will surely deliver at appropriate time of His choosing. It is always wise to have a close relationship with God at all times. Always remember God in good times so that He will remember you in bad times. Failure and disappointment come our way to help us realize our limitations and frailties, and the need to always rely on Christ.

Wives' Complaints about Husbands

1. He does not talk enough. He never talks to me any more.
2. He is lazy.
3. He is too tight with money. He always criticizes my spending.
4. He is a workaholic. He spends too much time on the job.

5. He is selfish.
6. He is not ambitious enough.
7. He does not compliment enough.
8. He does not want to go out.
9. He does not listen enough. He hears but does not really listen.
10. He does not take care of his health. You have to practically make him see a doctor.
11. He takes the wife for granted.
12. He leaves spiritual things to the wife.
13. He is not romantic enough.
14. He does not take time for the children.
15. He watches too much sports.
16. He is messy.
17. He is not sensitive to the wife's feelings.
18. He does not treat me the way he did when we were dating.
19. The only time he wants to be with me is when he wants sex. He only wants me for sex.
20. He does not allow me to have input on decision making. He makes important decisions without consulting me.
21. He does not help with household chores.
22. He spends more time with friends than he does with me.
23. He is too arrogant.
24. He spends too much time on the computer.
25. He does not make enough money. Therefore, she feels she must find a job to supplement the income.
26. He does not notice my new dress.
27. He does not notice when I do something new to my physical appearance.
28. Others appreciate me more than he does.

29. He is obsessed with television.
30. He is too controlling.
31. He rarely admits mistakes. He thinks he knows everything.
32. He is not patient with me.
33. He is not emotionally connected. He is obsessed with my body and not my mind.
34. He is not mature enough for me.

Husbands' Complaints about Wives

1. She is frequently late for appointments.
2. She talks too much. She talks too loud.
3. She spends too much money on shopping. She squanders family finances.
4. She does not praise enough.
5. She nags too much. She complains too much.
6. She criticizes too much.
7. She is selfish.
8. She is strong-willed. She does not listen to advice.
9. She is never satisfied. She expects too much.
10. She is too emotional. She is too sensitive.
11. She overreacts to everything.
12. She does not share the husband's sports interest.
13. She does not take good care of the home. She leaves shoes and clothes everywhere. She only cleans up when expecting company.
14. She compares me to another man.
15. She gives more time to the children than the husband. This is particularly true when newborns come.
16. She does not cook enough for me.
17. She is not sexual enough. She does not seem to enjoy sex like I do.

18. She wastes electricity and water.
19. She always wants answers right now. She is too impatient.
20. She only cares about the way she feels.
21. She shares family business with outsiders. She cannot keep a secret.
22. She is spoiled.
23. She depends too much on the husband.
24. She wants too much attention and affection.
25. She is too demanding.
26. She does not know when I need some space.
27. She is manipulative.
28. She does not keep herself looking nice like she used to.
29. She does not support enough.
30. She does not watch her weight.

Chapter Exercises

1. What do your marriage vows mean to you now that you are married?

> *Forgiveness is really something you do for yourself; it is a present you give to yourself.*

2. What do you understand about the permanence of marriage?

3. Do you think it is better to be married than to be single or unmarried? Why do you think so?

4. What do you think of Paul's advocacy for singlehood in 1 Corinthians 7?

5. Compare your love for each other now to that of your wedding night. What similarities and differences exist?

6. Will you say that your spouse is your best friend? Why or why not?

7. What is your attitude toward divorce and remarriage?

8. When can divorce be a good option for married couples?

9. What part does forgiveness play in a relationship?

10. Does forgiveness mean forgetfulness? Why or why not?

11. Discuss Christ's attitude on marriage, divorce, and remarriage.

12. How involved is God in your marriage?

13. Why do many marriages fail?

14. If you knew what you know now, would you have married when you did or would you have waited longer than you did? Explain your answer.

15. Do you have a living will? If so, does it specifically state how you wish to be treated if you suddenly become incapacitated by sickness, accident, or old age?

16. List some things you will do to improve your marriage.

> *Forgiveness is not a feeling; it is a decision, though very difficult at times.*

---

1. 1983. *The Holy Bible, New King James Version.* Nashville: Thomas Nelson Publishers.

9

Keeping the
Romance Alive

*We should measure affection, not like
youngsters by the ardor of its passion,
but by its strength and constancy.*

Cicero

Romance is one of the essential ingredients to a happy
marital relationship. The Bible even attests to this fact in
Song of Songs (Song of Solomon). Romance is another word
that means different things to different people. The best definition of romance is the one your significant other gives you.
Romance is whatever your wife or girlfriend (if you are
unmarried) thinks it is. Every lady has a vivid concept of
romance, and what is romantic to one woman may not be
necessarily romantic to another woman. When in doubt,
always ask your mate to refresh your memory. You might
even learn some new definitions. Romance is synonymous
with being a woman. Although a man desires a certain level

of romance, the woman needs more romance than her man. A man may go through life without it, but a woman may not.

It is appropriate to stress that it is common for a woman's preferences to change from time to time, depending on how she is feeling at the moment. A man can learn so much about his lady's preferences by simply talking to her at the feeling level. Ask her about her fantasies and what you can do to be affectionate to her. Even when a man wants to surprise his woman, it is still best to have a clear idea of what will really make her heart ecstatic. Should you decide to ask other people for suggestions, it would be wise to run the suggestions by her without being too explicit on what you are going to do; this will help you assess your options properly.

Some Things Couples Can Do to Keep Romance Alive

1. Regular dates together. Do something with each other at least once a week; this will enable you continue genuine courtship. You can have a weekly date night.

2. Share the day's activities with each other every evening. Be truly interested in your mate's daily activities, and show it by being an active listener.

3. Continue to compliment lots of things about each other both privately and publicly. Do not take each other for granted. Avoid slipping into a habit of criticizing.

4. Spend quality and quiet time together without the children, if any.

5. Give each other baths and massages.

6. Have weekends out of town together every now and then.

7. Write love letters and poems to each other. You can also mail a card to each other.

8. Dress to please each other and not the world. Remember that the way you dress is a compliment you give to your significant other.

9. Thank each other regularly. Cherish your lives together. Never miss out on an opportunity to express thanks to each other and to God.

10. Just talk to each other. Many problems are solved by simply talking about them. Talk sweetly to each other.

11. Keep personal hygiene at its best. This includes the sex organs as well. Body odor and bad breath are detrimental to romance. Feel free to wear your mate's favorite cologne or perfume, especially when you are intimate with each other.

12. Express love frequently. Continually tell your significant other that you love her or him. You can make surprise phone calls to each other during the day.

13. Be fully involved in the lovemaking experience. The level of involvement is normally determined by the way you treat each other all day long.

14. Watch your weight. Your appearance matters to your spouse. Do all you can to maintain your physical, emotional, and spiritual well-being.

15. *Surprise each other with gifts, flowers, and balloons every now and then.* Creativity adds a special touch to gifts.

16. *Both should stay close to God and serve Him always.* There is no substitute for this. A close relationship with the Lord will always put you on praying ground.

17. *Kiss each other regularly and passionately.*

18. *Do not ever put down each other, especially in public.* Avoid open disagreement with each other; some things are best addressed in private.

19. *Live below your means.* Your romantic live will be shattered if you continually spend more than you earn.

20. *Attend marriage enrichment seminars and retreats.*

21. *Go for a walk in the park.*

22. *Go to the gymnasium with each other.*

23. *Go to the beach or riverside to watch the sunset.*

24. *Prepare favorite meals for each other.*

25. *Never forget birthdays, anniversaries, and other special days.*

26. *Show affection even in public.* There is nothing wrong with holding hands or putting your arms around each other.

27. **Do things with other couples.** Be very selective in your choices. You want to associate yourselves with those who can help you improve your romantic live.

> *Romance is synonymous with being a woman. A man may go through life without it, but a woman may not.*

28. **Learn to enjoy the activities your mate is crazy about.**

29. **Read to each other.**

30. **Do not treat other people better than you treat each other.**

31. **Learn each other's love language and speak it often.**

32. **Do unexpected acts of kindness that demonstrate you truly know each other.**

33. **Be as courteous as you were while dating.**

34. **Go shopping together.**

35. **Reminisce on past romantic encounters.**

36. **Act out each other's fantasies.**

37. **Have a quiet candlelight dinner.**

38. **Spend a night in a hotel.**

39. Listen to soft music together.

40. Ask your mate if there are things you can do to be a better person for him or her. You might be surprised to learn about the little things that could help make you irresistible to your mate.

Chapter Exercises

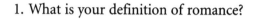

1. What is your definition of romance?

2. How will your significant other define romance?

3. Compare and contrast your responses with your mate.

4. What romantic fantasies do you have?

5. List all your preferred romantic ideas. Do it separately.

6. What can he do to be romantic and irresistible to you?

> *Every lady has a vivid*
> *concept of romance,*
> *and what is romantic*
> *to one woman may not*
> *be necessarily romantic*
> *to another woman.*

7. How can she help you to be more romantic to her?

8. Read the Song of Songs (Song of Solomon) together with your significant other.

9. What lessons can you learn from the wise man—Solomon—and his relationship with his bride?

10

Staying out of Financial Trouble

*Accumulating money is so easy, I'm surprised more
people aren't rich. That's the way money works.
The important thing is not how much money a person
makes, it is what he does with it that matters.*

A. G. Gaston

Many marriages end each year as a result of financial trouble. Money plays a very important part in maintaining a strong and happy marriage. Improper management of money or a deficiency thereof can easily weaken an otherwise strong union. It does not matter how spiritual you are, you are going to need some money to make it in your relationship. Every couple needs funds to be able to afford the basic necessities of life. The way one uses money reveals a lot about one's character.

Money is not a bad thing. However, the love of money will get one's focus off God and the significant other; this is when money becomes evil. Money is supposed to help us better serve God and each other. Money can either bless your relationship or it can create problems that never existed before. An insatiable appetite for it can alter everything, including the relationship with Christ and the spouse.

Finances should never be used as a means to control or mistreat the significant other, irrespective of which partner worked for the money. You cannot treat a thing, or anybody else for that matter, better than your significant other. The Lord cannot afford to accept second place on His children's priority list. Couples must ensure that nothing, not even the endless pursuit of money, takes precedence over God in their lives. Use the resources with which the Lord blesses you wisely, and He will be pleased with you.

Some Ways to Stay out of Financial Trouble

1. Budget: Couples should plan their budget before marriage; they should plan and practice living below their means. Make sure you have a budget that is strictly adhered to. There should be no surprises on the monthly bills. Learn to deny yourselves certain things when they are not really necessary or when the budget indicates the timing is not right.

2. Credit: Use credit only in real emergencies, and be wise about it. Limit the number of credit cards to one or two, and endeavor to pay up every charge at the end of the month. Avoid a high-interest credit card. A credit card is a trap; so do not be fooled. Credit should never be mistaken for a grant. It is a loan that must be repaid with interest; therefore, protect your credit. Get a credit card that is most suitable to your current needs.

3. Bill Payment: Always pay your bills on time. If there is any problem, notify the creditors before the payment due date.

4. *Shopping/Purchases:* Avoid impulse shopping. Make no private or controversial purchases. Learn to discuss with your mate before buying big items.

5. *Saving:* Learn to save for the unexpected contingencies. It is not always how much you make but how much you are able to save. It is fitting to always plan and budget for unforeseen life situations.

6. *Insurance:* Make sure you have reliable and reputable insurance. This includes health, auto, home, life, property, and others.

7. *Goals:* Establish short and long-term financial goals. Set a standard and measure your performance against the standard.

8. *Co-signing:* Be extremely careful if you co-sign a financial obligation for a third party, even if this is a family member. Remember that if the person defaults in payment, the creditors will be after you.

9. *Plan for retirement:* Do not live life like there is no tomorrow. Although God controls the future, He expects us to use the resources entrusted to us wisely.

10. *Charge for insufficient funds:* Be sure there are sufficient funds before writing a check or using your debit card. The bank charges $30 or more on each transaction, and you can save a lot of money by avoiding these unnecessary charges.

11. *Get a periodic credit report to check for inaccuracies and your credit rating.*

12. **Always shop around to obtain the best quote before signing up for any service,** be it insurance or buying or renting of a house or apartment, or even choosing an internet service provider (ISP).

13. **Minimize your ATM withdrawal.** It is always better to deposit more than you withdraw.

14. **Pray for wisdom to be prudent with money.**

15. **Learn to do minor housework and repairs,** instead of always seeking outside help. Take care of little problems or minor breakdowns before they escalate into major problems and expenditures.[1]

16. **Limit the number of long distance phone calls you make.** If you have a need to constantly make long distance calls, you might consider unlimited long distance offers by various telephone companies. You can also save by e-mailing or sending a card.

17. **You can save a lot of money by learning to cut or do your own hair.**

18. **Learn to negotiate or bargain when purchasing expensive items.**

19. **Limit the number of times you eat out,** and take advantage of two-for-one discounts.[1]

20. **Keep dating expenses within budget.**

21. **Think of things you can do together as a couple without spending any money.**[1]

22. Wait for discounts before buying things. There is nothing wrong with comparing prices at various stores.[1]

23. Double-check your monthly bank statements for errors.

24. Be able to distinguish between a need and a want. Sometimes people confuse wants with needs. There is nothing wrong with driving a used car if that is all you can afford. What you drive or wear is not who you really are; what you can afford is who you really are. Remember that everyone learns to crawl before walking.

> *What you drive or wear is not who you really are; what you can afford is who you really are.*

25. Avoid trying to keep up with the Browns and appearing to be better off, especially during the holiday season. It might be helpful to set aside some money every month in anticipation of holiday gift purchases.

26. Give as you prosper; this is very essential.

27. When filing for taxes, select the most beneficial filing status and claim all the deductions permitted by the law.[1]

28. Never get money dishonestly (Proverbs 13:11). God rewards honesty and hard work.

29. Use electricity wisely. Do not make a habit of leaving every light on when there is no need for that.

30. *Avoid wasting water,* especially hot water, when brushing your teeth or washing your face or hands.

31. *Never quit one job before finding another one.*

32. *Always plan ahead for vacations.* Get all the little things you will need prior to arrival at your vacation destination.[1]

33. *Renegotiate the interest on the money you owe creditors,* and request a lower interest rate.

34. *Debt consolidation* can significantly lower your monthly payment.

35. *Allow the one who is better at managing money to handle the finances.* However, both should learn money management skills. The husband is expected to know everything about his family's financial condition and consequently, he should make it a priority to learn working money management skills.

36. *Think of many other ways you can save money;* write them down, and put them into practice.

37. *Sometimes you may need an outside partner to help you assess financial preparedness.* Talk to others who know more than you do about money management. Do not hesitate to seek the services of a certified financial planner.

38. *Maintain self-discipline at all time.* Bear in mind that it is not always about how much money a couple makes;

sometimes it is more about what the couple is doing with its financial resources.

39. Be satisfied with God and each other. Do not hunger for the things that the consumer society seeks to create a hunger for. Be hungry for God, and your appetite will be less for material things that money can buy.

> *It is not always about how much money a couple makes; sometimes it is more about what the couple is doing with its financial resources.*

Do not forget to answer the questions at the end of this chapter.

Chapter Exercises

1. What part does money play in your relationship? Please elaborate.

2. What agreements do you and your significant other have on money?

3. List all the disagreements you and your mate have on money matters.

4. Do you have any financial plan? What does it entail?

5. What are your short-term financial goals?

6. What are your long-term financial goals?

Money can either bless your relationship or it can create problems that never existed before. An insatiable appetite for it can alter everything, including the relationship with Christ and the spouse.

7. Should couples have joint or separate bank accounts? Explain your rationale in detail.

8. What will you do if you had to choose between feeding your family and giving to God's treasury?

9. If you had a million dollars today, what will you do with the money?

1. Nardini, J., & Meyering, A. (2002). *600 simple tips to save you money.* Nashville, TN: Premium Press America.

11

Managing
In-Law Problems

*"No one can serve two masters. Either he will
hate the one and love the other, or he will be devoted
to the one and despise the other. You cannot
serve both God and money."*[1]

Matthew 6:24

It is suitable to stress that no one can love spouse and parents to the same degree. A married person cannot give his or her heart to two services at the same time. Not only is this an impossible mission to accomplish, it violates God's principles on marriage. Many spouses experience resentment and unhappiness because of allowing in-laws into their private business. Couples need to do some leaving before cleaving, and they should note that the interest of the spouse takes precedent over that of parents and any other person on earth.

The intervention and involvement of in-laws can have serious and harmful ramifications in a marriage, depending on the absolute maturity of the couple involved. The practice to

> *Many spouses experience resentment and unhappiness because of allowing in-laws into their private business.*

involve one's parents (in-laws) in marital problems does not only depict immaturity and irresponsibility, but it also shows selfishness on the part of one extending the invitation. Every time a couple involves a third party in its problems, the couple misses a grand opportunity to grow and glorify God.

Leaving parents, brothers, sisters, uncles, and aunts, and cleaving to the spouse means that couples should learn to work out their difficulties and not cultivate a habit of running to in-laws (parents) every time there is a problem or disagreement in the marriage.

The husband and wife must surely recognize that the mate comes first in his or her life. If anyone is too dependent on his or her parents, it will invariably lead to serious problems. It is always very difficult for in-laws to be objective. It is basically believed that parents will be partial toward their offspring in the marriage. When this is the case on both sides, it will exert tremendous strain on the marriage. It is safer to seek a counselor that can be impartial and objective in serious disagreements on various things.

In many cases, involving a third party in a marital problem, especially your own family members, leaves the two of you worse off than you were prior to the involvement. If you have to talk to a third party about your problems, it is always wise to select an older couple that both of you admire and respect. The two of you must agree to involve this couple. Make sure that you can trust the couple with your problem. Always pick a couple that is not only more experienced than you are but will also give you God's perspective in solving your problems.

Most mothers tend to hold to their children more than fathers; however, there are exceptions to every rule. When parents think objectively, they realize that in their own marriage there were periods of adjustment where they had to work through serious problems. Many times it is wise to listen to advice from faithful people, but the final decision should be between the husband and the wife even over the objection of their parents and others.

Be very careful about comparing your spouse to your parents or other family members. This can be devastating, particularly if your remarks extol your parents at the expense of your spouse. There is nothing wrong with admiring your parents and aspiring to achieve the status they have achieved, if they have or had a god-fearing relationship. The problem is using your parents as an example to prove a point every time something goes wrong in your marriage relationship. When you do this, you put your spouse in an uncomfortable and defensive position, and problems that never existed before may begin to surface. Remember that in-laws and other third parties cannot be involved in your relationship unless you allow them.

Some Ways to Deal with In-Law Problems

1. *There needs to be closeness but mutual respect.* Establish early in the marriage that the partners are committed to each other, and that in-laws are respected but not necessarily obeyed. The blood relative should be the one to explain your rules of intervention and involvement to the blood relatives.

2. *Grandparents are normally good babysitters.*

3. *Use in-laws for wisdom, counseling, family history, and nurturing.*

4. Stick to the Bible, *"leave and cleave."* No marriage can succeed without strict adherence to this principle.

5. View in-laws as total family. Appreciate them as the family system God used to shape, mold, and develop your spouse. They should be viewed as in-laws and not out-laws.

6. Avoid sharing your problems with them. Keep them out of the marriage. Remember that you and your spouse are one and not many.

7. Do not live too close to them. Live far away and visit infrequently. Allow son or daughter in-law to decide on lengths for visits.

8. Never talk negatively about your spouse in the presence of your parents or other family members. Do not put down your mate's family, even when you are upset about something.

9. Resolve to never allow anyone to control your relationship.

Chapter Exercises

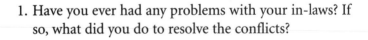

1. Have you ever had any problems with your in-laws? If so, what did you do to resolve the conflicts?

2. What are some of the major reasons couples encounter problems with in-laws?

> *Every time a couple involves a third party in its problems, the couple misses a grand opportunity to grow and glorify God.*

3. Do you currently have any issues with your in-laws? If so, what are they?

4. What does your spouse think about the problems you are presently experiencing with his or her parents (family members)?

5. If in-laws were influencing your children in a negative manner, what would you do?

6. What does it mean to leave father and mother and to cleave to your spouse?

7. List all the things couples can do to resolve in-law problems.

It is always very difficult for in-laws to be objective.

1. 1991. *Life Application Study Bible*. Wheaton, IL: Tyndale House Publishers.

12

What It Means to Truly Love a Person

Love is patient, love is kind. It does not envy, it does not boast, it is not proud. It is not rude, it is not self-seeking, it is not easily angered, it keeps no record of wrongs. Love does not delight in evil but rejoices with the truth. It always protects, always trusts, always hopes, always perseveres. Love never fails...[1]

1 Corinthians 13:4-8a

Love is a word that is sometimes used loosely. You cannot love sports or going out to eat the same way you love your significant other. Love, when applied to a person, should have a deeper meaning. Marital love is exclusively for the two people involved; it is selfless, pure, and holy. There are many forms of love, but the emphasis in this book is on *eros, philia,* and *agape*—the three forms of love essential in a marital relationship. Each of the three types of love is sequentially discussed below.

It is the belief of many that the first love that develops when a man and a woman first meet is *eros*. *Eros* is a romantic or sexual love.[3] Sometimes it is referred to as love at first

> *Marital love is exclusively for the two people involved; it is selfless, pure, and holy.*

sight.[2] You probably experienced instantaneous attraction for each other when you and your significant other first met. The feeling of attraction might be so strong that it becomes lust. At this time, you realize it is time to take your love to another level. In any successful marriage, it is necessary for the couple to love each other romantically. Erotic partners usually anticipate a monogamous relationship with their spouses; love immediately becomes sour when one party cheats on the other.

The next form of love is *philia*. This is friendly or brotherly love. In a great marriage, the man and the woman are also best friends. It was stated earlier in this book that a friend loves at all time. When spouses are also best friends, they will always protect one another's interests. The husband and wife need each other's companionship to be able to enjoy marital bliss to the fullest.[3]

Of all the three forms of love, *agape* is the most essential in marriage and Christian relationships. This is selfless or unconditional love; this is the kind of love that is most needed to build a relationship. Those in *agape* love do not expect everything to be 50/50; they are always ready to do for the other person before they do for themselves, no matter the situation. They realize that every day is not going to be the best day, and that there will be ups and downs. Agape lovers recognize that they will not have perfect happiness and conflict-free relationship all the time; they believe in giving, building up, and forgiving. Christ best exemplifies *agape* love in His daily treatment of humanity. His love for the Church is also a supreme example of *agape* love. When you genuinely love your spouse, you will be willing to give your life for the spouse.

To truly love someone is to always put that person's best interest ahead of your own interest. It means you do for the person before you do for yourself and feel good about doing it. Before you make a decision, you assess its impact or possible impact on the one you love. If making a particular decision will negatively affect him or her, you reconsider what you plan to carry out and may examine an alternative course of action. You are willing to sacrifice yourself unconditionally for the other person because you love that person. To truly love someone is to do things that make life better for that person. You like things about him or her, and you care for the individual in sickness, health, good, and bad times. You are always looking for opportunities to praise and lift up that person. True love keeps no record of negative behaviors or wrong doings; it accepts the other person as he or she is. There is a genuine commitment to please each other when a couple has *agape* love for each other.

> *Agape lovers recognize that they will not have perfect happiness and conflict-free relationship all the time; they believe in giving, building up, and forgiving.*

True love is reciprocal; it is not a one-way street. Love responds to love. One must give love to know how to receive love. It is more satisfying to give than to receive love. It is impossible to be a good lover without being a good giver;

love is always giving. Love is helping the significant other grow and mature in the spiritual life. It is assisting the other person in overcoming his or her weaknesses and faults. Love is speaking the truth without condemnation and criticism. Love upholds the marriage vows. Someone once said that love is making a fool of yourself for someone else; this may be true during the early days of courtship. However, true love from another person eliminates the need to act like a "fool."

> *True love is reciprocal; it is not a one-way street.*

When you love your significant other, you will respect, honor, adore, care for, protect, defend, talk to, spend time with, share with, show kindness to, be sensitive to, laugh with, cry with, help, work with, tend to, and be patient with him or her. When you love your spouse, you will treat the spouse as yourself; you will honor and cherish the spouse as he or she is, making room for individualism; you will place the spouse above all others; you will trust the mate; and you will feel incomplete when the spouse is not present.

There are different levels of love, but *agape* love will endure anything. When a couple loves God and only then, can each really love the other. Love grows as couples go through the good and bad times. They learn to appreciate each other more when they remember where they have been and how far God had brought them. When you love your significant other, you will enjoy growing old with him or her. True love demonstrates itself by the way one thinks, feels, and acts.

Please do not forget to complete the exercises.

Chapter Exercises

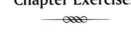

1. How will you define love?

2. What is your significant other's definition of love?

3. Explain the following from 1 Corinthians 13 and give some examples:

    A. Love is patient.

    B. Love is kind.

C. Love does not envy.

D. Love does not boast.

E. Love is not proud.

F. Love is not rude.

G. Love is not self-seeking.

H. Love is not easily angered.

I. Love keeps no records of wrongs.

J. Love does not delight in evil but rejoices with the truth.

K. Love always protects.

L. Loves always trusts.

In a great marriage, the man and the woman are also best friends.

M. Love always hopes.

N. Love always perseveres.

O. Love never fails.

1. 1991. *Life Application Study Bible.* Wheaton, IL: Tyndale House Publishers.
2. Lasswell, M., & Lasswell, T. (1991). *Marriage & the family.* Belmont, California: Wadsworth Publishing Company.
3. Wright, H. N, & Roberts, W. (1997). *Before you say "I do."* Eugene, Oregon: Harvest House Publishers.

13

God's Design
for the Family

*"Unless the Lord builds the house,
its builders labor in vain."*[1]

Psalms 127:1

The home is the earth's oldest institution. The significance of the family cannot be adequately emphasized. God recognized the importance of the home from the beginning of creation. The Lord, indeed, has a design for the family; He set forth His plan for the home in no uncertain terms. With all of the creatures, God made male and female from the beginning. When God made man, He made man alone in the beginning and then observed him.

It is evident that God had thought of a creature that would complete man, but it was as if man was put under observation for a time. Then God said, "it is not good for the man to be alone. I will make a helper suitable for him"[1]

(Genesis 2:18). With the oldest and greatest of all operations, God took a rib from man's side and made woman. God brought the woman to the man and apparently gave Adam a reason to rejoice when he said, "This is now bone of my bones and flesh of my flesh; she shall be called woman, for she was taken out of man"[1] (Genesis 2:23).

The man will cleave to his wife and the two will become one flesh. It is clearly evident that God wanted this unit intact before children would be conceived and borne within the confines of that family entity. It is rational to build a solid relationship with the spouse before the arrival of children. It would be unwise to plan for having children when the marital relationship is on shaky ground. Work on the relationship and ensure a strong union between both of you before children arrive. Husband and wife have different roles but the same goal of pleasing God to go to Heaven.

Being the head means the husband should be the service pioneer for the family.

The man is the head of the home as Christ is the head of the Church; the wife will be submissive to him, especially in things that are right (1 Peter 3:1; Ephesians 5:22-25). A god-fearing wife should never have any problems submitting to her husband, particularly when the husband also submits to God; this should be the case even if she is making more money than he does. Every organization must have a head to maintain order; there will be lawlessness in the family if everyone wants to be the head. Submission is used positively; it does not mean inferiority or master-slave relationship. In fact, both the husband and wife are to be mutually submitted to each other.

The husband is commanded to love his wife as Christ loved the Church, and the wife is commanded to obey this loving husband as doing it to please the Lord. She should recognize the man's authority as the spiritual leader of the family. Being the head means the husband should be the service pioneer for the family; this means he models a life of selfless services to his family. Role should never be equated with significance because the husband and wife are equally significant in the sight of God.

The family structure has been recognized as the backbone of the Church and society when it follows God's orders. Different families make up the Church and society; therefore, what affects the family also affects the Church and society. The home is an institution that impacts the Church and society the most. Children are told to obey their parents in the Lord because it is the right thing to do, and parents are advised not to aggravate their children. The parents should teach and display Christ to their children; they should also discipline them without hesitation. This can mean using the rod appropriately. Discipline should never be done out of anger. When these three (husband, wife, and children) follow the Lord's directives, there will be no problem in the family. Although the home is daily threatened by societal forces, families still have to adhere to God's commands. Leadership in the home will be thoroughly discussed in the next chapter.

> *The man is the head of the home as Christ is the head of the Church; the wife will be submissive to him, especially in things that are right.*

Chapter Exercises

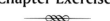

1. What does it mean to be a helper or helpmeet?

2. What are the fundamental functions of the home?

3. What should the wife do in a situation where the husband is deficient in spiritual leadership?

4. Assuming the husband is leading according to God's plan, what should he do if the wife refuses to submit to his leadership?

5. What can he do to make it easy for her to submit? Be specific.

6. What do you make of God's design for the home?

7. What does it mean to be the head?

> *When these three (husband, wife, and children) follow the Lord's directives, there will be no problem in the family.*

8. Explain what the word *submission* mean to you?

9. When is the education of a child completed and the parents' responsibilities over?

10. Is it wrong for married couples to reverse their respective roles as was designed by God? Are there exceptions? Please explain.

11. What roles can the Church play to help families reach spiritual maturity?

---

1. 1991. *Life Application Study Bible*. Wheaton, IL: Tyndale House Publishers.

14

Leadership
in the Home

*It is the price of leadership to do the things that have to
be done at the time they have to be done.*

President Lyndon Johnson

In a world where men bashing has become the norm, it is appropriate to remind all men that they are a very special group of individuals with a special responsibility to God and their families. It must be stressed that it will be extremely difficult, but not impossible, for the man of the house to be all that the Lord intended for him without his lady's undying support and encouragement. No leader can reach the fullest potential unless he learns to motivate himself. Leadership is a responsibility that is placed on the husband and father in the family. Every father is a male, but every male is not a father. A person is not a man because he can make a baby; a person is a man because he can take care of one. No innocent child should be brought into this world if the child cannot be provided with the basic necessities of life. These necessities include not just food, clothing, and shelter; it also includes guidance and admonition in the ways of the Lord. The future of every family, society, and organization hinges on strong male leadership. The fewer the fathers in the families, the wilder the children will become. This is not to downgrade the noble work done by women on a daily basis, but rather to demonstrate that both men and women have different roles in God's order of things.

> *Every father is a male, but every male is not a father. A person is not a man because he can make a baby; a person is a man because he can take care of one.*

The man does not only produce, he also provides for his family spiritually, psychologically, monetarily, and futuristically. Before any man can qualify to be a husband and a father, he should have a job and a place to stay. Not only does he produce and provide, the man also protects his family. He must be alert at all times. He needs to know everything that goes on in his family. This includes the kind of television programs they watch, the kind of books they read, and the kind of conversation they have.

The husband is supposed to spend enough time to really get to know his wife, and he should always be understanding of her sophisticated nature. The wife must reciprocate this gesture by recognizing that her husband is unique and different from any other man, and she should concentrate on things that make it easy for him to be a leader that God brags on.

A good leader must first of all be God-centered. He must have integrity. A good leader is one with a tender heart and not a loud mouth; he gives more of his heart and less of his mind. The leader

> *A good leader must first of all be God-centered.*

dominates the environment and not his fellow man. He has the courage to say what needs to be said (the truth) in love. The test of leadership is the ability to make things better than they were previously. A leader has the capability to motivate people to do things they would not otherwise do. There is no such thing as a born leader. True leaders are molded and not born. God endows every man with at least one talent, and the man has sole discretion on what he chooses to do with the talent or talents. We tend to take so many things for granted, especially if we did not work for them. This is even true in our relationship with Christ. When a man develops the talents he possesses, he is expressing a deep gratitude to God; he is also qualifying himself for more blessings from the Lord.

A great leader always seeks the opportunity to serve others. He initiates good things and sets an excellent example. The leader must lead with a loving attitude because he has the fear of God in him. A leader invites his family members to join together in something good, and he is proactive in nourishing a healthy relationship. The great leader will always take the initiative to work out difficulties when they arise. He guides his family spiritually, emotionally, socially, and financially. A good leader will usually make all decisions with his family's best interest at heart. The leader supports meaningful cause even if the idea did not originate with him. He is firm but fair; he is understanding and aware of his family's needs. A godly leader will never give up on his family, no matter how difficult things are at the moment. A woman might be able to quit her job, but a good leader will never quit one job before finding another one because such a decision may be financially traumatic for his family. A man who wants the best and is not afraid to sacrifice for his family will not take such a risk.

As the leader of your family, there will be times your wife may not agree with you on essential matters. Although the two of you may disagree on some occasions, that does not eliminate the fact that a decision or decisions still must be made. It is always essential for the leader to involve his family in decisions that will impact their lives. There will be times when the leader will have to make some tough decisions alone. However, he must exhaust all avenues for consensus decision-making prior to deciding alone. The man has to decide based on God's word and on what is best for his family. Selfishness should never be the reason for making any decision regarding our families. The Lord will hold the man accountable if he does not lead his family according to His plan. It does not matter how visionary a man is, the vision becomes useless unless it is based on God's plan.

> *A godly leader will never give up on his family, no matter how difficult things are at the moment.*

Husbands should not be frustrated when they cannot get their wives to view the future like they do. Most women are not programmed to process information and to think like most men. Men and women sometimes process information differently. Your wife may not agree with many of the decisions you will make as the man of the house. However, she will appreciate you more when everything turns out right. A good example will be planning for the children's future before they are born. This is not to imply that there is something wrong with your woman's thinking because that would be the farthest thing from the truth. She thinks and decides the ways she does because she is more of a feeling being.

> *It does not matter how visionary a man is, the vision becomes useless unless it is based on God's plan.*

One of the great qualities of a leader is the ability to make the right decisions under the most tedious circumstances. As a leader, you have a God-given responsibility to protect your family's future. This is not to say that you have absolute control of your family's future; it means that just having faith in God without doing what you are supposed to do is not enough to make your dreams come true. Good things come to those who believe and also work hard for them. Idleness is the quickest route to poverty, and the surest way to failure is the temptation not to do anything at all about our circumstances in life. Without today's plan and action, there is no tomorrow's dream realization. Even if the wife focuses on the present, the husband should focus on more than the present; he should also have a clear vision of the future. Sometimes it is necessary to experience short-term discomfort in order to obtain long-term comfort. A family's future becomes doubtful when the leader stops being visionary.

Being the leader does not make me better than my wife. Being a leader means that I team up with my wife to carry out God's plan for our lives. Teaming up means recognizing her talents to the fullest. A great leader is never afraid to admit a mistake. He knows his limitations and when to delegate. Leadership is not dependent on title or position in your job or in society. Leadership is commitment. Leadership is responsibility. Leadership is serving. Leadership is giving. Leadership is patience. Leadership is loving. Leadership is courage. Leadership is God-fearing. Leadership is Heaven-bound. My family is my first church and ministry. If I fail to serve my wife and family at home, it makes me a hypocrite to serve others while my family's needs are unmet. My greatest responsibility as a leader in my home is to lead my family to God. I must be able to provide the tools and environment to get the family to meet Christ in peace. It does not matter how much God helps me to achieve in life; I will be a great failure as a leader and as a man if I fail to lead my family to Heaven. You will be bountifully blessed by God when you lead well.

> *Idleness is the quickest route to poverty, and the surest way to failure is the temptation not to do anything at all about our circumstances in life.*

Please remember to do the chapter exercises.

Chapter Exercises

1. What is your definition of a leader?

2. What is your significant other's definition of a leader?

3. What key qualities should a leader possess?

4. Name one person you admire as a leader? How well do you know this person? What makes him a great leader?

5. Name ten things she can do to help him lead according to God's plan.

> *There is no such thing as a born leader. True leaders are molded and not born.*

6. Read Proverbs 31:10-31. What can you learn from this noble woman as a couple?

7. Discuss Moses and Joshua as leaders of God's people in the Bible.

8. Evaluate Christ as the best leader of all time. What can you learn from his style(s)?

The future of every family, society, and organization hinges on strong male leadership.

15

Finding and Keeping Your Significant Other

"Do not be misled: Bad company
corrupts good character."[1]

1 Corinthians 15:33

Throughout this book, the author has consistently stressed the importance of establishing and keeping healthy relationships. The significance of being engaged only in relationships that are sanctioned by Christ can never be exhaustively emphasized. The kind of relationships people choose to be involved in can determine the kind of life they live here on earth and where they will live when this life is over. Stop dating people you do not like. It is irrational to date someone you would not want to be married to.

It is also a waste of valuable time and energy to initiate something with a person of the opposite sex you can never see as a potential mate. Be very careful because it is possible to start liking just about anybody when you continually do things with that person. You will gradually see yourself enjoying the company of a person whose character and attitude will be damaging to a marriage. Do not allow yourself to be emotionally connected to someone who has nothing beneficial to offer you. One can easily fall in love with the wrong person, and it is often very troublesome to terminate a relationship if one of the parties is still hanging on to it. Do not learn simple life lessons the hard way. You can learn so much by simply watching others who had already made some serious mistakes in choosing their mates without having to experience the same thing.

Finding Your Significant Other

Deciding on the person to marry is perhaps the most crucial and difficult decision you will ever have to make. Choosing right may be the difference between happiness and misery. No one is right for you if the person is not right with God. You cannot serve the Lord appropriately if your house is not in order. You want to marry someone who will encourage you to do things that are pleasing to Christ. Do not rely on your own strength to make the right decision. You cannot pick the right mate without the Lord helping you. Pray incessantly to God for assistance and believe that He will assist you.

Do not set a timetable for God. The Lord does not always respond when we want Him to respond. God operates according to His timetable, and He is always on time. Many times we have to patiently work hard to obtain the best things in life. Do

> *No one is right for you if the person is not right with God.*

not look for mastery as you search, look for potential; look at the big picture. Look for someone who loves God more than any other person. The person will be there for you because the integrity is in him or her. Take all the time you need; it is better to be late than to be sorry. It is critical that you keep your eyes open; then proceed carefully in your choice. The author strongly recommends that a Christian should marry a Christian for reasons discussed earlier in the book. If you are looking for a potential mate, it makes sense to go to all the places you can find the kind of person you are looking for. If you want a Christian spouse, it will do you much good to look in all the right places. Some happily married couples met their mates in Christian schools, singles' retreats, church fellowship, through a mutual friend, and others met while on trips to places of interest. Do not limit yourself to your local church; visit as many congregations, events, and places as possible. Unless you get out of your comfort zone as you search, you may miss out on what God has in store for you. The more exposed you are, the better your chances of finding a desirable potential mate.

> *Do not look for mastery as you search, look for potential; look at the big picture.*

The Lord helps those who help themselves. God will provide opportunities and will make ways from no ways. People have a responsibility to take advantage of all the avenues granted by God for the betterment of His creation. Faith without works is dead. Although God presents us with numerous opportunities in life, the final decision on what to do with those opportunities is ours alone. This applies even when one is single and searching for a potential life companion. The Lord will answer your prayers by helping you find someone that

> *Although God presents us with numerous opportunities in life, the final decision on what to do with those opportunities is ours alone.*

could potentially become your mate. However, the choice on whether you want to develop any relationship with this individual is yours and yours alone. God made us free moral agents and will never take away our freedom to choose in life.

Many people are single today because of the choices they have made in life. Sometimes people go through various rejections before finding their significant other. Remember that everything worthwhile normally comes with a price, and every decision we make has consequences. We should have the courage and comfort level to live with all the decisions we make in life. We should always pray to God to guide us into making the right decisions at all times.

Be very careful about saying that it is not God's will that you should be married. Does it mean that God loves others more than He loves you? Absolutely not. God is always just, and He does not show favoritism. He loves all of His children equally. The author strongly believes that if you honestly seek first the kingdom of God, the Lord will bless you with other things you need. Although Paul—the Apostle—advocated single lifestyle, he cautioned that it is wise to marry to avoid fornication and constant burning with sexual desire (1 Corinthians 7). God does not will that any of His children should live in sin and as such will offer every opportunity to find a mate to one who sincerely and prayerfully desires a lifetime partner. The problem, many times, is not that the Lord does not respond to His children's prayers for marriage partners; the problem, sometimes, is that many people refuse to take advantage of different opportunities provided by the Lord to meet and maybe establish a meaningful relationship that could possibly culminate in marriage.

Many times people think that they know the kind of individuals that will complement them as mates. However, God always knows what is best for us. We need to learn to set our standard according to God's standard. This does not mean that you settle for second best. Go for the very best in life, and the Lord will make your goals realized. When you pray to God for what you need, assuming that you are living right and not doubting that the Lord will grant your request, the Lord will definitely grant your request. It might not be the kind of person you are praying for and it may take years, but God will always respond at the time and manner of His choosing.

It is good to always view one's circumstances through the eyes of faith. Develop the kind of faith that sees the invisible, the kind of faith that conceives the inconceivable, the kind of faith that believes the unbelievable, and the kind of faith that moves God to compassion and action. There is no room for doubt and pessimism when dealing with Christ. Your faith can be so strong that you practically believe something into existence. If you never see yourself somewhere, you will never get there. Never quit hoping in God. Hope is the best antidote for weariness; it makes life worth living even in crisis. When people stop hoping, they stop living. Hope in God helps one to face today, and it also provides the courage to face tomorrow. Hope comes only by seeing the Lord's perspective.

> *Hope is the best antidote for weariness; it makes life worth living even in crisis. When people stop hoping, they stop living.*

God always determines when we are ready for something. Never give up on God. He can do without us, but we cannot do without Him; we need Him all the time. Bear in mind that the Lord will not bless you until you are fully ready to receive His blessings. When God gets ready to bless you, no person or force can be powerful enough to hinder your blessings. God gives freely to those He loves and because of His nature, the Lord wants everyone to be blessed. However, it is critical to note that our actions or inactions can delay or block our blessings. When other people are blessed, do not get upset; thank God for them because yours is just around the corner. Approach the Lord constantly with your request and patiently wait for His response and deliverance. What God has done for others, He will do for you. You have to believe that God's promises are true because the Lord cannot lie.

Keeping Your Significant Other

People from all walks of life dream about meeting their soul mates. Sometimes they get their hopes so high that they become unrealistic and unreasonable. Even when you meet your perfect match or ideal person, there are going to be significant differences between the two of you. Many times the differences are not obvious until you become husband and wife. Regardless of how much you have in common, there will be some dissimilarities between you. These differences are not necessary bad, and dwelling on them can be poisonous to your marriage. Differences will enable you to see the other person's perspective, and they will also help you to think outside the box.

> *Your faith can be so strong that you practically believe something into existence.*

Focusing more on the things you agree on and learning to celebrate your differences will contribute significantly to happiness in your relationship. Before Adrianne and I got married, we liked many of the same things; we thought alike in many respects, and we had and still have the same religious beliefs. We even used the same hair lotion and lip balm years before we met. As our marriage continues to grow, we realize how different we are in our thinking. We, however, agree on things that matter.

> *In a relationship, there will regularly be something that the two of you are working on.*

When you first meet a prospective mate and even after you have been married for some time, it is very unlikely that both of you will always be on the same level of development at all times—both on spiritual and non-spiritual matters. It is incumbent on the one who has reached a desirable level of development to learn to wait on the one who is trying to attain this desirable level. The one that has not yet attained the appropriate level of development should work at getting there. In a relationship, there will regularly be something that the two of you are working on. You might be strong in one area and weak in another area. This is the reason it is crucial that you help each other to reach your fullest potential. It is not abnormal for the two of you to be on different levels of development at times. In fact, this should be expected before and after you have been married. What makes the real difference is a constant commitment to make your relationship be the best it can possibly be.

There might be times you cannot even stand to look each other in the face, especially in the early days of your relationship. However, as time goes on and you grow together, many of the things that used to bother you either will not trouble you anymore or not as they used to. You begin to look at things from a different perspective. You reevaluate things and begin to ask yourselves, are all of these worth giving up the special relationship we have? You might be disappointed in each other every now and then, but you learn to grow through your disappointments. Remember, in a relationship, both of you will not be at the same level all the time. Now that you are married, you must make the best of your situation to keep the relationship growing and stable. God ordained marriage for a lifetime.

Sometimes people think that retirement takes effect right after the wedding, and that one does not have to work as hard as one did before the marriage. The problem is that you do not operate in a dream world but in a real world. In order to keep your mate happy, you must continue to do those things you all did to attract each other before the wedding. Once you are married, you work harder and not less than you did during dating period. Do not be afraid to try new things with each other. Remember that anything estimable normally takes some time to accomplish. You will need to spend a lot of time to really get to know each other. You will make several mistakes along the way, but let each mistake or disappointment help you to be a better husband or wife. Always keep God alive in your marriage.

Please respond to the questions at the end of the chapter.

Chapter Exercises

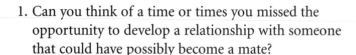

1. Can you think of a time or times you missed the opportunity to develop a relationship with someone that could have possibly become a mate?

2. What did you do to drive this person away?

3. If you had the opportunity again, what will you do differently?

4. Make a list of where you can go to increase the chances of meeting the kind of individuals you desire as a potential mate.

5. What will you do if you were to meet this special someone today?

6. Why do you think you are ready for a serious relationship?

7. What does it take to keep a relationship growing?

8. Are you absolutely sure that you have what it takes to keep a relationship? Be true to yourself.

9. How do you feel about women courting men?

It is relevant to note that we are not always in control of our circumstances or misfortune in life. However, we are always in control of our response to whatever happens to us. You cannot control the way the other person is going to treat you, but you can definitely control your reaction to the way you are being treated. Remember, kindness breeds kindness. My best wishes in your relationship. With Christ, everything is achievable; without Christ, nothing is achievable. When we genuinely humble ourselves and recognize our need for God, He will come to us and exalt us.

---

1. 1991. *Life Application Study Bible*. Wheaton, IL: Tyndale House Publishers.

Appendix A

How Well Do You Know Your Significant Other Questionnaire

1. Where did you meet your mate?

2. What was the first thing you said to him or her when you first met?

3. What did you do on your first date?

4. Where did you go on the first date?

5. What is your mate's idea of a vacation?

6. When it comes to planning for vacations, do you or your significant other normally take the initiative?

7. Where were you when you proposed to your spouse?

8. If your significant other had one wish, what will it be?

9. What is the silliest thing you have ever done?

10. What are your spouse's parents' full names?

11. What was the name of your mate's first date prior to meeting you?

12. Where was your significant other born?

13. What time was he or she born?

14. What was the weight at birth?

15. What concerns your spouse the most about his or her appearance?

16. What is your significant other's favorite food?

17. What is his or her favorite restaurant?

18. What is her favorite dessert?

19. When it comes to shopping, would you classify your mate as a conservative or big spender?

20. Does your spouse have a favorite movie of all time? If so, what is it?

21. Does he or she prefer warm or cold weather?

22. Would you classify your significant other as more of an introvert or an extrovert (reserved or outgoing)?

23. What is your spouse's favorite season?

24. What sport does your spouse enjoy playing the most?

25. What sport does he or she enjoy watching the most?

26. How does your spouse respond to open criticism?

27. Is it easy for your mate to ask for help when needed or will he or she quietly hope others will notice the need and voluntarily assist?

28. What will your significant other likely do if his or her feelings were hurt?

29. How does your spouse deal with stress?

30. How does your spouse feel about politics?

31. What does your mate like to do with his or her spare time?

32. What does your spouse enjoy most about holidays?

33. Will you classify your significant other as easygoing or strong-willed?

34. What is the wildest, most adventurous thing your spouse would like to do?

35. What animal is your spouse most afraid of?

36. What is your mate's favorite Bible verse?

37. What is his or her favorite television show?

38. Is your significant other an indoor or outdoor person?

39. What is your spouse's most annoying habit?

40. What habit does your mate find most annoying in other people?

41. What were your spouse's favorite subjects in junior high school?

42. What classes did your spouse dislike the most in high school?

43. What do you remember most about his or her college experience?

44. What is the most embarrassing thing your mate has said in public?

45. What will make your significant other really feel special?

46. Name two of your mate's favorite hymns.

47. What will you consider your spouse's greatest achievement?

48. Name the household chore your mate dislikes the most.

49. What character in the Bible best describes your mate? Why?

50. What will he or she consider a typical day?

51. What size of shoes does your mate wear?

52. What is your spouse's favorite cologne?

53. What cologne or perfume did your mate wear today?

54. Describe your significant other in five words.

55. How tall is your spouse? Be very specific.

56. What does your spouse like most about you?

57. What do you like most about your spouse?

58. What is your mate's favorite love song?

59. What character on the TV does your spouse admire the most?

60. Why do you think your spouse really cares about you?

61. If your mate had a million dollars today, how would he or she spend the money?

62. Name the top five things that are most important to your spouse.

63. If you had a very bad news for your spouse, how do you think he or she would prefer you deliver the news?

64. What attracted you to your mate when you first met?

65. How old was your spouse when he or she learned to drive?

When you finish, compare your answers with your significant other's. How well did you do? Do not be discouraged if you score low; it only means that you have some work to do.

☐ 65 (Excellent)

☐ 60-64 (Very Good)

☐ 50-59 (Good)

☐ 40-49 (Fair)

☐ 39 and below (Low)

Appendix B
Index

About the Author

D r. Etido Oliver Akpan has several years of relationship-building experience. He has worked with singles and newlyweds for many years. Dr. Akpan's experience transcends cultural, educational, socio-economic, national, ethnic, and religious boundaries. The author holds a Bachelor of Business Administration in Management, Bachelor of Science in Bible, Master of Business Administration in General Business, and a Doctor of Business Administration in Information Systems. Dr. Akpan is currently a full-time professor of business and information technology at Strayer University. He is also an independent business consultant. His family comes before his career. He strongly believes that the quality of relationships people have in their personal lives will greatly impact the performance in their professional lives.

Dr. Akpan is also the author of *Strategic Alignment: A Business Imperative for Leading Organizations*. The author and his wife, Adrianne, are happily married. They have two children, Etido Jr. and Abigail. It is the author's belief that this book will be a great resource for all those that desire to make the best in their relationship. The book provides instantaneous help to those engaged to be married, newlyweds, struggling marriages, and others in relationship with the opposite sex. Dr. Akpan welcomes your feedback on this book.

Please feel free to include suggestions for improving the next edition of the book. You can write to Dr. Akpan at: P. O. Box 252 Cordova, TN 38088. The author also encourages readers to visit his website to be kept abreast of his appearances and publications. — www.DrAkpan.com

Finding and Keeping Your Significant Other
Order Form

Postal orders: P.O. Box 252
                            Cordova, TN 38088

E-mail orders: www.drakpan.com

Please send *Finding and Keeping Your Significant Other* to:

Name: _____

Address: _____

City: _____ State: _____

Zip: _____ Telephone: (_____) _____

Book Price: $16.00

Shipping: $3.00 for the first book and $1.00 for each additional book to cover
shipping and handling within US, Canada, and Mexico.
International orders add $6.00 for the first book and $2.00 for each
additional book.

Or order from:
ACW Press
1200 HWY 231 South #273
Ozark, AL 36360

(800) 931-BOOK

or contact your local bookstore

A portion of Dr. Akpan's proceeds will be donated to charities.